How To Get Girls

The Definitive Guide

Charles
Sledge

Table Of Contents

How To Get More Ass Than A Toilet Seat

How To Be A Natural With Women

3 Lies That Men Believe About Women Debunked

Can You Seduce A Woman With Eye Contact Alone?

Always Be Willing To Walk Away

Women Want To Be Objectified

All Women Are Insecure

Women Are Easier Than You Think

A Simple Word That Is A Guaranteed Panty Dropper

Why You Should Smile & Make Eye Contact With Every Attractive Woman You Pass

A Principle To Always Keep In Mind When Seducing Women

Naked Desire

Why You Should Never Hide Your Interest In A Woman

Is Desire The Key To Game?

A Simple Mind Trick That'll Have You Getting Laid Like Tile In No Time

How To Use Emotional Spiking To Get Laid

Introduction

Attraction. What was once a simple and straightforward process has been turned into something resembling a Frankenstein like rocket science. Except unlike rocket science this was designed to simply lead you around in circles not take you into space. Between Feminists, the "pick-up artist" industry, corporations pushing products, and the emasculation of the American male what women find attractive has become an extremely confusing topic for the average male.

Men are told conflicting and downright horrible advice as to what will attract women to them. From women want a "nice, sensitive guy", to buy our car or cologne and the women will flock to you, to memorize these weird tricks and gimmicks to manipulate women to sleep with you…sometimes. And much much more. It's gotten out of hand.

Despite popular belief attraction is not only a simple process but a natural and easy one as well. It doesn't require years of effort to get good with women. And anyone who tells you that it does, doesn't know what they are talking about and frankly I wouldn't listen to that person's advice on women.

A man's desire to have sex with many beautiful women is perhaps his largest driving force in life, other than basic water, food, and sleep. When you look around at society the vast majority of us have our basic needs such as food, water, sleep, and shelter met. To varying degrees but nevertheless the desires are met. Yet when it comes to having the sex life with the women they want, the vast majority of men fall short of what they can accomplish. It would be like most men desiring millions but surviving on minimum wage and being okay with that.

You should never settle as a man. This is something I try to hammer home in all of my books. There is no need to settle in any part of your life. Your love life is no exception.

Regardless if you are married and wish to ensure that the flame remains strong between you and your wife or you want to become the next Don Juan this book will put you on the path to accomplishing your goals. What turns women on does not change once a woman has a rock on her finger. Her feminine nature remains the same whether she is just graduating high school at the age of eighteen or becoming a grandmother at the age of sixty five. Women are women.

The principles lain out here work on women. They are what women naturally, biologically respond to. A woman cannot control whether she responds to these things or not as they are innate. They are not negotiable. Women will become irresistibly attracted to you when you embody the principles lain out in this book. Doesn't mean it won't take work or time. Depending on where you are it make take both. But the important thing is that you will be on the right path and headed in the right direction.

You won't have to go from scam to scam or from bad advice to bad advice. You will have the truth and the truth will set you free. No longer will you have to wonder if you will ever achieve the love life of your fantasies. You will, trust me.

You may think that you are a special case. That yeah this might work for the average guy but not for me. You're wrong. If you are a human male this will work for you. It doesn't matter if you are fat, a virgin, or anything else you think might limit you. These principles are timeless. As long as humans remain humans these principles will work.

You have been lied to. You have been told that what attracts women is relative. That women are now attracted to sensitive guys or whatever the trend of the day is. If you've been around the block awhile you know that this is wrong. You may not yet know what does attract women but you are aware of what doesn't.

Like everything society has played a large role in getting you to believe certain things. Frankly it is not in society's best interest if you get laid a lot. It isn't in the best interest of those in power if you lose your chains in any part of your life. Whether it is finances, political thinking, or just thinking in general. Your love life is again not an exception.

If you spend your time making money, enjoying life, getting laid, and learning useful things it's very hard for you to become a drone, to become a worker bee. It's harder to make a freeman a slave than it is to make a slave free. Those who are in control know this.

Some men achieve freedom in many areas of their life such as finance, societal conditioning, their belief system, yet still remain slaves when it comes to beliefs in what attracts women. I've said it before and I'll say it again women can either be one of the greatest sources of pleasure and fun in your life or one of the greatest sources of pain and heartache in your life.

All depending on if you know how to handle them or not and if you understand what causes attraction. After reading this book you will have both more than handled. What was once unclear to you will begin to make sense. Like a ray of sunlight piercing the fog.

Your relations with women are an important part of your life.

There is no denying this and there is no way around it. Which is fine, women were meant to be, were created to be a part of a man's life. Whether as husband and wife or as a king with his harem. Men and women were created for each other. To enjoy each other. Obviously a great many stops and hindrances have been placed between the sexes since that time in the garden but they can be overcome by exposing those lies designed to divide the sexes to the truth.

What attracts man to woman has been true since the inception of man and women and will remain true until the extinction of man and women. Like the universe is guided by certain laws. The law of gravity, the law of cause and effect, and so on and so forth. So is attraction between the sexes guided by timeless laws set in place to aid us.

Begin your journey into the truth and your life will forever be better for it. Each chapter is a part of a whole. There isn't any "Read this one chapter for this routine then go out and use it". Rather like a jig saw puzzle (with each chapter representing one piece) you will only get the full picture when it's all together. Also you'll notice that many principles are repeated throughout the chapters. This is no accident. It takes the average person 18 times hearing or reading something before they get it completely. Repetition aids in learning.

If you have read the blog then you will be familiar with much of the work here. But like stated above you never fully get something going over it one time. Through repetition you get to a deeper and deeper level of understanding until it becomes a part of you and you don't even have to think about it. That is my goal with this book. To have the principles become a part of you so you naturally attract all the women you desire in your day to day life. All through having the right beliefs and taking the right actions. Now without further ado let's go ahead and get started.

The Sexual Pyramid

No this isn't a weird sex move. The sexual pyramid is the sexual hierarchy. A hierarchy that most choose to ignore yet nevertheless affects their day to day lives. Nature is hierarchical and while we may be able to deny hierarchy in things like rights, employment, and other areas but this illusion will cause you nothing but pain when you apply it to a biological function like mating.

Now when looking at human sexuality we're going to have to generalize when coming up with models to represent it. The sexual pyramid is a base model, not perfect by any means. However it does a great job of conveying a sexual truth. And yes there are such things as sexual truths.

Alright before we dive in let me address some issues you may have. Some people think that dating and mating are things that cannot be understood and therefore usually result to platitudes like "be yourself" or "you'll eventually find the one" and unless you're a hot girl these things will never work. Human sexuality is something that can be understood just like anything else. No one has to go around not having the success with the opposite sex they want, they chose to.

For example is someone is having trouble with their finances do they just throw up their hands and exclaim "It's impossible to figure out!"? Alright some people do and those people are called poor people. Smart people go and buy books, watch videos, talk to experts until they come away with an understanding of what it is that is frustrating or confusing them.

However when it comes to dating most people, especially men, think that their "luck" with women will never change. Despite the fact that like getting rich "luck" has very little to do with it. Alright if you want to start on your journey to improve your dating life then keep reading what this book has to offer (as well as my other books which all aid with this in one way or another).

Now the sexual pyramid. We'll divide it into three sections the top, the middle, and the bottom.

The Bottom

The bottom are those with the least amount of sexual options. The ones that fall into this category are the majority of men and ugly/overweight women. This tier makes up the majority of the population. Most people simply put are not attractive. Doesn't mean their bad people just that their not attractive people. Now even though overweight and ugly women are the bottom of their respective sex as far as mating desirability goes they still hold a higher spot on the bottom tier than the majority of men do.

Why is this?

Now there have been a number of "studies" done where multiple dating profiles are put up on a dating website of both men and women. The men and women ranged from very attractive to downright ugly. Let me ask you a question who do you think got more responses? The ugliest women or the best looking men? Go ahead and guess.

Did you guess?

The winner is…the ugliest women. That's right the worst looking of the women still got more responses than that best looking of the men. Now does this mean that ugly women occupy a higher spot on the sexual pyramid than good looking men? Not necessarily so for reasons we will get to in a bit. However this does illustrate a point. As far as getting attention from the opposite sex goes women are going to have a much easier time, however for attraction quality attention that is a different story.

Mid-Tier

Alright the mid-tier is made up of all the rest of women who are overweight or ugly. Again this is not a judge of anyone's personal character. But remember biology has no moral compass to it, it simple is. Now the rest of women is a pretty large group.

It is. The best looking women are at the top of the mid-tier and the not so good looking ones at the bottom. Yet all women are contained here.

Most people who imagine that beautiful women would occupy the top of the pyramid but that is not so. Now if looks were the only category for sexual selectivity then yes they would and if women had the same sexual selection process as men then again yes they would but this is not so. Men and women look for different things in a sexually suitable partner. Translated to what turns women on is different from what turns a man on.

And just for future reference no women are not attracted to sensitive nice guys (but they're really easy to use).

Top of the Pyramid

You've probably heard the statistic that "20% of men sleep with 80% of women" while obviously getting exact measurements on this will never happen I think this statement is more on less true (give or take a couple of percentages). Point is guys who get laid a lot, get laid A LOT. And guys who don't get laid a lot, don't get laid a lot. While women occupy a place somewhere in the middle.

So for sake of simplicity let's say that the average number of partners the top tier has is ten, the middle five, and the lower one.

You see how this can translate to society. You have the player asshole who has had sex with five girls who all ended up marrying some nice guy whose virginity they took. Or something similar. These girls will usually lie to the nice guy about their past to make sure he doesn't feel bad but the alphas at the top tier all know the truth about women's sexuality.

What does this mean for the average guy?

Now if you're a guy I think it's safe to say that the top 20% (or 10%) is where you want to be.

Am I right?

Of course I am.

So why don't more guys end up there? Simply put they don't know that they can. They think that their place on the pyramid is something that is static but it isn't it is dynamic. Just like someone can rise from poverty to riches so can one rise from dud to stud. Granted that they are willing to put in the time and effort. Nothing happens on its own.

The reason I brought this up is to show men two things

1. women do not hold all the power sexually

2. you place on the pyramid is not static but dynamic

I hope that this knowledge gives you hope. For those of you who wish to ascend to the top of the pyramid not just in sexual desirability but across all aspects of life then keep reading (as well as check out my other books which as I said all aid in becoming a top level man).

Sometimes Girls Just Want Sex

Sometimes you're just at the right place at the right time.

A lot of guys think that they have to do all these different things to get a woman to come home with him. Display high value, make her laugh, etc. etc. However this isn't necessarily the reality. Oftentimes a girl just wants a guy. She just wants to get laid. It could be you or the next guy. Whoever has the balls essentially.

Understand this <u>sleeping with women is not a complicated activity.</u>

Alright?

There are no sequence of magic words you must say. Or a particular set of things that you need to go. Sex is a natural activity, a biological activity. It's not complicated.

A lot of guys think that girls are all about relationships, romantic love, and commitment. But this is not the truth. Women get horny too. Women want sex too. They are human just like men. Sometimes they just want a guy to screw their brains out. Nothing more and nothing less. A lot of guys can't wrap their heads around this. And that's unfortunate for them.

Sex doesn't have to be a big deal. Women will go with the frame that you present them with. Women are followers by nature. Men are leaders by nature. A woman will follow whatever frame you present to her. Meaning if you go up to a woman and make it seem like sex is a big deal she's not going to see you as a fun guy to have a one night stand with.

Meaning if you're one of those guys who says "Oh yeah guys who just want sex are pigs", "No I wouldn't have sex with a girl the first night I met her, I respect women", "I'm a little bitch". You get the idea. Being dishonest about what you want from a girl will not get you anywhere.

It's Okay To Want Sex

You are after all a man. Women expect this from you. Generally the women who complain that men are just about sex are the woman who aren't getting any or at the very least not getting good sex.

Humans are sexual creatures. They want sex. Social pressure is essential placed on women so people don't spend all their time screwing and actually get things done. Think about it, imagine if women who slept around were also considered "studs" or whatever the female equivalent is. Nothing would get done because everyone would spend their entire time having sex.

So instead society tells women if they have sex they're bad and tells men that if they want to have sex with women they're pigs and misogynistic. Obviously this is nonsense. Men and women were created for each other. They are perfectly designed for each other at a fundamental biological level. They can't help but be attracted to one another and want sex with one another.

You see this is something that happens naturally. Most guys let their societal hang-ups get in the way of them getting laid and having the sex life that they want. Remember sometimes girls just want sex. Sometimes girls just want to have some fun. It could be with you or the next guy, they just want a guy who's not a complete creep. Which you are not.

Get out of your own way.

Don't Over Complicate Things

Sex and seduction is a <u>simple</u> and <u>natural</u> act. It's not complicated. This doesn't mean that people don't understand it. Because most don't. Between societal influence, the media, and the education system what is normal is completely warped and destroyed. Things that come naturally are restrained and controlled. You are told natural feelings and desires are bad. For one simple reason, so you can be controlled.

This isn't an conspiracy it's simply what makes sense. If you have all the power trust me you would use every tool at your disposal to stay in power. Society is no different. They want people to be controlled so that they are more useful to those in power, no matter how it affects the individual's life. One thing that must be controlled is people's sexual drive.

So understand why this is. Don't get mad about it. Just understand it and then do your own thing.

And Remember

Sometimes girls just want sex.

Attract Don't Pursue

What does this mean?

Put simply it means that instead of chasing women you become the kind of man that women chase.

Simply put but how do you get there?

Invest In Yourself

First and foremost you must invest in yourself. You must take care of yourself and believe in yourself. If you don't treat yourself well then others are not going to. And no woman wants to be with a doormat, whether it's her own personal doormat or a doormat for others.

By building yourself up through investing in yourself you will naturally become more attractive to women. By putting yourself first women will become more attracted to you. Because they will know that you are a man who is confident and has self-respect.

Getting women is a by-product of being an attractive man. Being an attractive man has little to do with outer traits. Such as looks and money and a hell of a lot more to do with inner traits. Such as confidence, masculinity, decisiveness, and so on and so forth.

This is something that takes time and is a constant ongoing process. There never comes a time when you should stop growing, stop getting better, or stop investing in yourself. However don't think you need to become some sort of superman before women will chase you, nothing could be further from the truth

First and foremost don't think women are any better than you. I don't care if she is Miss America and your a drunken slob who lives with your parents. If you don't think a woman is better than you than that will show in your interactions with her. Nothing repels women more than needy and desperate men. And one of the top things that conveys neediness is thinking that a woman is somehow "above" you. Don't ever let yourself fall into this line of thinking. No woman is better than you, no matter what. This doesn't mean you need to go around thinking you are better than all women are treating them like crap just don't ever think they're better than you.

Now about how you can produce this vibe even without building yourself up first. Although ultimately you should be doing both.

Focus On Yourself

Focus on yourself and on thing you can control. When you go out don't desperately try to get the attention of all the women there. This is lame and will make women more turned off if anything. Do your own thing. Have your own fun. Focus on having a good time and creating a memorable experience for yourself. Don't focus or worry about the women there.

When you are doing your own thing and having fun, women will naturally be drawn to this. You will be carefree and not be focusing on them. Because of this they will want to see what you are all about.

Be your own personal party. Whoever comes into your zone is going to have a good time because your focus is on creating a good time for yourself. Not for others, not for the women, but for yourself. When you are care free and having a good time women are naturally going to match your emotions.

Women often act like mirrors reflecting whatever you are projecting back at you. Meaning if you are fun loving and having a good time the women around you are going to have fun and have a good time. They going to naturally match the emotions of the man they are around or with. Granted that he is a man and not a wimp.

You've probably seen this before. The guy who is surrounded by women yet could give a damn about them. Sure he might take one (or two) home but his focus is on himself and having a good time himself. He has a carefree, fun, and relaxed attitude. He projects a "I don't give a damn vibe". There is no doubt in anyone's, especially attractive women's, mind that he loves himself. People are drawn to individuals who love themselves.

The key here is to be comfortable. To essentially be yourself, your true self. To express that without giving a damn what others think. You must feel good yourself and then that will naturally be expressed to others and rub off on them. Focus on the things you can control, such as having a good time and don't worry about the things you can't control like the other people wherever you are at. Have fun don't worry about others, including hot women.

If you feel like you need the girl you will never get the girl. Have fun with every girl regardless of how they look. Don't treat attractive women any different than you would their plain friend. This will make you even more intriguing as most attractive girls are used to being worshiped. Even though they often eventually resent their worshipers.

A Caveat

Do your own thing yet don't forget at some point you may want to pull a girl.

So don't completely ignore a girl if she is in to you and you are in to her. Use common sense. At some point if you want to take the interaction forward you must take actions to do so.

Focus on yourself, on having fun, and on having a good time. Don't make focus on a woman/the women.

Include girls in your vibe and if they don't wane or like it then move on. Easy as that.

Focus on yourself and the things you can control and let the rest go.

How To Approach Beautiful Women

At some point a man gets tired of meeting women through friends, circumstances, or family and decides to take matter into his own hands. However most men end up snagged on the right way to do this. First off there is no "right" away and as long as a man is taking action he is on the right path. Second off this is something that should be a straightforward and easy process not something that people write whole books about (though I'm sure some do).

Approaching a woman is not rocket science or hard. It will go against your social conditioning at first but after a while you we become immune to it and have no hesitation when doing it. However there a couple of things to keep in mind that will make things go smoother and cut down on your learning time. Keep these few things in mind next time you see a pretty girl and approach her.

You're The Man

You are the man. Don't forget this. When you approach a woman do so as a man. Be forward, bold, and ballsy. Not crude or inappropriate but unapologetic and straightforward. Don't hesitate or hew and haw. Take action and be direct. Don't be coy. A woman knows why you approached her. While you don't have to make a huge deal out of the fact that you are attracted to her, make sure that is known beyond just talking to her. You not relating to her as friend to friend, as gay to girl, or girl to girl. You are relating to her as man to woman which means there is sexuality in the mix.

Women want men. They are attracted to masculine confident men like you are attracted to women with round asses and perky tits. Don't get it in your head that you are undesirable to women or that they don't want to be approached by men because they do. They may test you at first but if you hold you ground and <u>be a man.</u> They will melt before you.

You're Already More Than Enough

You are not approaching a goddess or a divine being you are approaching another human being. Another human being with insecurities and faults. You do not have to be perfect the fact that are taking action already makes you stand out from the majority of men who will never take action. They will just sit back and watch as opportunities and life pass them by. There is no such thing as being "good enough" for a woman, you are already more than good enough. You are already more than enough.

A man seeing an attractive woman and going up and talking to her is natural. It isn't weird or wrong or misogynistic/sexist/evil/etc. It is normal and natural and anyone who thinks otherwise is the one with the problem not you. We do not live in a healthy or natural society don't curb your life to fit in with what society wants. Doing what is right and what is good often goes against what society wants. What women want sure as hell goes against what society wants, that's for sure.

Attitude

This is the attitude that you should have that the woman that you are approaching is lucky to be approached by you. This doesn't mean you act like you are better than her especially if it is coming from a place of insecurity it will shine through and you will come across as a try hard. No, what I mean by this is that you are a man who appreciates her femininity and are man enough to initiate the interaction to see where it will lead. This type of man is rare and women appreciate it, unless they have issues and if they do they generally aren't worth your time anyways. Note: Many women have issues so don't be surprised at the weird reactions you may get. Hold the frame and be a man and things will turn out for the best.

Your attitude or inside is always shining through. Your mindset is always shining through. That is why one guy can walk up and say something weird and corny to a girl and have her laughing and smiling. While another guy can walk up to a girl and say something nice yet get an eye roll or a brush off. Girls can pick up on your inner attitude and since the feminine is reactive in nature, it will react to it. Be genuine with girls. Genuine means being real about your desires and be unashamedly a man. Again doesn't mean you have to be crude, just real.

Remember

1. You're the man, act like one

2. You're already good enough for every woman on this earth, never think otherwise

3. You inner attitude is always shining through, be real

Remember these three things and you will save yourself a lot of time and frustration.

5 Reasons Why You're Not Getting Laid

Not getting laid. Every guy pretends like this was never a problem for him. "Yeah man I walked out of the womb pulling nine's left and right" bullshit. At some point in our lives we have all had to deal with this. Most guys are not having the sex life that they want. This is a simple fact. A simple fact that most if not all guys will ignore, deny, and/or cover up. Not getting laid for a guy is like being a slut for a girl. They do everything they can to hide it.

Hiding a problem does nothing to solve it. Many guys are more concerned with being "cool" to other guys than they are with having an awesome sex life with beautiful women. This is lame and a little gay. If you're sex life isn't where you want it to be it will bother you. You shouldn't concern yourself with what other guys think. This is something I've said before especially in my books but it bears repeating. Most of humanity is like crabs in a bucket. Every time one begins to rise up the rest drag him back down. Below I'm going to cover the top five reasons most men aren't getting laid.

Reason #1 – You Hide Your Desires

"Go talk to that girl" "Nah man" "Why not?" "She's ugly" "You've jacked off to porn three times in the past week shut the fuck up and go talk to her". If only we all had such honest friends. Next time you go to a club/bar or where ever look around you at the men. What are they doing? Most of them are standing in circles or against the wall like scared puppies and if you asked them why they were there what would they say? "Just here to chill man" "Just out with the guys" alright if that's true that's cool but it's not true and we both know it.

Most guys are afraid to admit
that they want to get laid because
they are scared it will make them
look like they don't get laid. A little
ironic right? If you pretend like you
don't want to get laid you're not
doing yourself any favors. Be okay
with your desires they are natural
and normal. Don't worry about
what others guy will think. The
ones who will judge you probably
aren't having the sex lives they
desire either.

Reason #2 – You Have No Game

This is another key reason why
guys aren't getting laid. Because
they have no game. While game is
something that can be overblown

(especially if someone has something they want to sell you) it is a fundamental requirement to getting laid like tile.

What is game? Game is simple knowing what is attractive to women and utilizing it. You can get laid without game no doubt, game just simplifies the process and makes it much easier on you. Learn what turns women on and how to do it and you'll be making it much easier on yourself. Reading this book will take care of that.

Reason #3 – You're Not Going Out

If you don't go out you won't get laid. You could have the looks of Brad Pitt and the charisma of James Bond and still be a sexless virgin if you don't go out. You have to go where women are to have sex with them. Sounds simple but so many guys will only go out one night a month or go out with the purpose of day gaming once a month and then wonder why they are barely getting laid (if at all).

You need to get out and around women often. Would you expect to go to the gym one time and have a body you were happy with? No of course not. Having a great sex life is no different. Sure once you've gone out awhile you can establish yourself a harem but you must crawl before you walk son.

Reason #4 – You Don't Believe That You Can

Ah belief, the keystone to everything. You've probably heard the famous Henry Ford quote "Whether you think you can or think you can't you're right". Truer words have rarely been spoken. Without belief you might as well give up and go home. Mindset is everything. With it there is literally nothing you cannot do (except violate the laws of time and space) without you can do nothing. I cannot stress how key this is. We've all seen some guy who gets laid a ton or makes a lot of money and you and everyone around is just like "WTF…" or "Why?" or "How?". Usually this kid has the right mindset.

Reason #5 – You Get Sloppily Drunk

Look I love my whiskey like any other red blooded man. But there comes a point where getting drunk works against you instead of for you. If you get drunk to the point where it's hard to talk you're going to have a hard time communicating to women. Here is why we drink because it frees our social inhibitions. But you can be free of your social inhibitions without alcohol and take time and work (cue horror music) but it can be done. You just have to work at it. It takes time to break free from the social programming but it is oh so worth it.

Summary

So remember don't be afraid of your desires. Learn some game. Get out of your house and meet women. Believe that you can get laid (this is so key). And finally stop getting so drunk, get over your social inhibitions the healthy way. Through pushing yourself in day to day situations

Women's Biology The Source Of All Their Behavior

All of a women's behavior stems from here biology and desire to survive and reproduce. Unlike in days of past when human (especially female) sexuality was constrained now with no constraints biology has been able to run wild. In essence the law of the jungle is in effect. What this means is that males who operate on old standards such as women will be loyal if you're married, if you provide for her, or simply because society would shame her otherwise have all gone away. This frees women's sexuality to do as they please. If you are a man stuck in an old paradigm you will get screwed by this. However this can also work to a man's advantage. Read on.

Evolutionary Biology

A woman's mating strategy is dualistic which simply means that it has two main goals. One is to be provided for and the other is to foster good genes so that her children will go on to reproduce. These aren't things women consciously think about but unconsciously. Just like when a man sees a woman with a nice ass he doesn't think "Damn those hips are perfect for birthing a child" it's the same with women. This happens on a unconscious level. In ancient times men who were good providers often were also the dominant males. The best hunter in the pack would also have been the one who took the most risks and asserted himself. However in the modern world things have taken a drastic turn.

Alpha Fucks, Beta Bucks

Now men generally fall into two categories. You have the stable nice guys who lavish women with gifts and generally have stable careers to support a woman yet aren't very manly or dominant, these men are generally referred to as betas. Then you have the other men the "bad boys" who treat women like crap and simply pump and dump them, these men are usually swarming with women yet at some point women realize these men aren't going to support them, these men are generally referred to as alphas.

So women's sexual strategy calls for women having their cake and eating it too. So what most women do is get a beta man who will provide with them and they generally marry these men. Then bang whatever alpha happens to come along and turns her on enough. Thereby fulfilling the need for provision and the need for good manly dominant genes. Most would say what about morality or faithfulness or love? My response would be you must not know women very well. Even when society heavily regulated female sexuality women still could not deny their attraction to alpha men. Even when adultery was punishable by death women still couldn't deny their lust for alpha men. Now that all societal stigma and negative consequences have been waived for women who stray they are free to pursue their sexual strategy to the max.

What This Means For You

Never has it been better to be a man in the alpha category and never has it been worse to be a man in the beta category. Read that last sentence again. It's very important and the main point I want to get across from you. Luckily for you being a alpha or a beta is a choice. It is something that you can change. Simply by becoming aware of this strategy you automatically get a leg up on the vast majority of males in society. Many who will blunder on thinking marriage or providing for a woman will keep then loyal. When it will do anything but.

Women's first and primary goal is good genes providing for her or not treating her like complete dog shit is a nice bonus. I'm not saying to treat women like dog shit what I'm saying is that if you're alpha that's generally all a woman is going to care about. Hence you have the mass murderers and sociopaths who women literally throw themselves at and you have the hardworking doctor working on a cure for cancer who's first wife left him for a man that beats her every night.

So Remember…

Just like you can't help responding to a thin waist and a

nice round ass women cannot help but respond to men who are masculine and dominant. It isn't a choice. Those are the two things women look for you. You could be an ugly, drug addicted, wife beater yet you would still get more women than the stable, faithful, loyal doctor. Because when it comes to attraction none of those traits that doctor exhibit do it for a woman. As a man (especially if you are a young man) focus on being masculine and dominant then add in the other traits and never expect a woman to respect or want you for those other traits.

How Women View Men

Now that you understand a bit about women's biology it's time to talk about how women view men in terms of that biologically programming. Women divide men in different categories which serve different functions for them. You've probably heard about the lover and provider categories. Where a woman will shack up with a rich man who supports her while getting her rocks off with the biker at the local bar type dynamic. Meaning that women see some men as men they want to fuck and other men as targets to support them. Or Alpha Fucks, Beta Bucks put another way.

I once read a very insightful quote that read.

"Women's hindbrains are constantly scanning for alpha, tolerating beta, and ignoring omega"

This quote is very enlightening and reveals a fundamental truth about the nature of woman and hypergamy. Become an alpha and women will fall at your feet, be beta and they will take advantage of you, be omega and they won't even realize that you exist.

Scanning For Alpha

A woman's brain is always trained to look for a dominant masculine man. A man who fully embraces his masculinity and makes no apology for it. The type of man that give women the tingles and turns them on. Women cannot help but be attracted to men like this and nothing will get in the way of them wanting men like this. Especially not things like being provided for and taken care of, having a beta (or even less alpha) husband, or their own personal reputation.

These are men who exists at the top of the sexual hierarchy and sleep with the majority of women. Two traits that generally make these man stand out from others is their unapologetic attitude and their dominance. Two traits that are too women what the sight of crack is to an addict. Women are always (and I mean always) on the scan for men like this. It's in their nature and they cannot help it. Doesn't matter if their on a date with a guy (or their husband), running errands, or with their children they stop and notice when they see an alpha. Like a gazelle picking up a strange scent on the savanna.

Tolerating Beta

Next are the beta males. These men come in many shapes and sizes. Despite popular belief many rich and good looking men are in this category. Men who think money is all women care about and that hitting the gym is the best way to get women fall into this category. Women love these men for one simple reason, they are easy as hell to manipulate and use for their own ends. Beta males believe in the framework of society that women would have them believe. One prime example is that women love money.

Don't get me wrong women are attracted to men with money.

But only so they can take that money and then if they feel like they can get away with it screw real men on the side. Money doesn't turn women on but it is useful to them and they will exchange sexual favors and attention for a beta male to bestow money on them. However women usually get sick of beta males because their not fully masculine and will jump at the chance for an alpha if the opportunity ever arrives.

Ignoring Omega

Omega men are the nerds and what society calls "losers". The men that expect to be ignored by women and who often are. Women could often care less if all these type of men died and often wouldn't notice it if they did. Women have no sympathy especially for a male who can't be a man. Understand this. While women may find weakness and cluelessness cute in babies and young children they find it repulsive and disgusting in full grown males.

These men often suffer from lack of attention and would do anything for a woman's attention. However because they are not masculine and offer no utility women want nothing to do with them. The alphas turn them on and the betas have their uses but the omegas do nothing for them. Women make fun of them and ridicule them mercilessly caring little for the consequences. These are the type of men when combined with certain drugs go on shooting rampages.

Women...

Know this women are one hundred times more heartless and merciless to males who cannot be men. If a man cannot embrace his masculinity women will detest him for it even if they don't know why. Sure they will say how brave he is and how good he is but when it really comes down to it they loathe men like this. They may tell how their husband does the dishes and how great that is yet deep down they hate his guts for not putting her in her place.

Never has it been better to be an alpha. While alphas have always had top access to women now it skewed even further in favor of the alphas. Also it has never been worse to be a beta or an omega. Be an alpha an all women will want you married, dating, young, old, think, thick, rich, poor it doesn't matter, you're alpha.

Women Want To Be Led

Women love dominant, masculine men. Men who are strong, men who are men. Just like men love women with tight waists and round asses. This is a fact of life. A law if you will. And like all laws of nature you can only crush yourself against them, you cannot change them. It doesn't matter how strongly you want to believe in something like Feminism it isn't going to make it true.

One thing that society has pushed is that women want to be leaders and that as a man to lead a woman is somehow wrong. Yet like just about everything pushed by society this is a lie done for ulterior motives. If you read The Primer you know that society often does not have your best interests at heart (if ever). Base your life on what societies says you should and you'll end up another sheep. Miserable while being led to your slaughter. Base your life on the truth and you will be able to make what you wish out of your life as you will have a solid foundation upon which to rest it.

One of these truths is that women want to be led by a man. Or one of the sexiest things you can do with a woman is lead her.

Leading Is A Form Of Dominating

Despite what society says women don't want to be the leaders or the bosses. They have an innate need and desire to submit. They want to submit yet in today's world are rarely given the opportunity to do so. Which often leads to frustration and anger. When a built up need is not met or not fulfilled resentment and anger build up. A woman wants you to lead her, she wants you to make the decision and set the direction in which you go.

Women thirst for being led and dominated like men thirst for young blondes with tight waits and firm asses. They don't want to make the decisions and set the precedent that is your job as the man. Man is the head of the relationship, regardless if that relationship is a marriage that lasts until death or a twenty minute bang after meeting in the parking lot. Another thing that adds to the sexiness of being led (for women) is that it is not expected. In a society where men are castrated and neutered at every turn a man with his balls in tact is a rare commodity indeed.

There are many places to lead women and ways to do so here are two of the best.

In Life Goals

While I'm not saying you should explicitly chart the course of a woman's life when it comes to setting the direction for your family or a relationship with a woman you as the man are the one who should do so. If you and a woman are sitting down and discussing what the direction you want to head in is, it is the man that should have the lion's share of the say. It doesn't matter if this is setting down career goals or which path to take in the woods while camping. The man should set the precedent and have the final say. This doesn't mean to not listen to the woman, simply that your decision is the final and most important one.

I see many men when discussing things with a woman (especially if this woman is their significant other) to defer the decision making for her. "What will our careers look like in five years honey? asks the woman "Whatever you want hon" replies the man. And the woman loses attraction and respect for the male she is with. She wants direction, she wants to be led.

Physically

"Let go to the dance floor" I grab the woman by her hand and lead her out there. Meanwhile her eyes light up and she can't stop smiling. An act simple as that can change a woman's entire demeanor. When you want to take a woman somewhere do so. Don't ask, take her by the hand and tell her where you are going. Trust me they more often than not will follow both happily and willingly.

This applies doubly to the bedroom. You must take a woman and ravish her. Do the opposite of the slow gentle love making you see in cheesy movies. Take a woman and have your way with her animalistically and primally. As a man taking and ravishing a woman. Lead her, do with her as you want. Don't expect her to take the lead in any part of the interaction. The feminine is reactive while the masculine is active.

Remember

Women want to be led. Despite what society and others say it is a biological truth. And biological truths cannot be undone. Lead her, she will be grateful and turned on by it. Women were made to be led by men and for men. She doesn't want to be the decision maker and she doesn't want to be the leader. As the man that is your job.

Two Things That Matter Most To Women

Many men are often surprised when they hear about the things that women will do with other men. Often boyfriends and husbands will lament how their women will not X, Y, or Z with them when they have done it with other men, some within a few hours (if not less) of meeting them (often the boyfriend and husband have no knowledge of this). Other men believe that you must go on x number of dates with a woman before you can have sex with her or that there are certain time limits on what you can do with a woman.

Hell there are some men out there who think you have to date a woman before she will sleep with you. Society combined with women pushing B.S. to protect their reputations has led to many men believing in many falsities when it comes to having sex with women. While it would take multiple volumes to address all of them rather I want to highlight what to do push past (or completely avoid) all of these.

If you are an attractive man, or an "alpha". Women are going to behave much differently with you than with other men. While they will make other men wait to kiss them if you do the things below they could be riding you within an hour of meeting them (if that is what you want). Put simply women cannot control their sexuality around dominant masculine men. Even when society has severe restrictions against female sexuality the restrictions still were no match for a woman's biology. Women are always on the lookout for a guy who gives them the "tingles" (aka turns them on).

Take The Responsibility

A woman (unless particularly slutty) isn't going to take the responsibility for sex. She is going to want you to take it and as a man it is your job to (if you want sex that is). You must take the responsibility for the interaction and whatever happens in it. This provides her with a disclaimer and thereby can keep her reputation in tact (which is what a woman cares about anyways).

When you take the responsibility she can say "It just happened" or "I was swept up in the moment". Women want to avoid all responsibility for whatever they do. As eternal children they seek to maximize their fun while minimizing their responsibility for any consequences that that fun may bring about. As long as she can "blame" it on you on something else she'll do whatever. If she can get away with it without getting caught a woman will do anything you want her (or she wants) to do.

Discretion

In addition to taking responsibility for the act you must also be discreet. No woman wants to be the girl that some insecure guy brags about banging to all his friends. Men who are actually good with women know that one key is to keep everything on the down low. In other words don't kiss and tell. What happens between you and a woman stays between you and a woman. Don't share all the intimate details with your friends and never share names. Once a woman knows she won't end up the topic of conversation next time you and your buddies are having some drinks she'll be much more open to indulging in her desires with you.

Like I said men who are good with women don't brag about every time they have relations with a woman. Men who feel like they have to brag about every woman they have sex with are men who aren't getting very much action. Keep what happens with a woman between you and that woman. As long as you keep everything between you and the woman she will do whatever you want and love every second of it.

Remember

What matters to a woman is her reputation. Unlike a man a woman doesn't care about her actions as long as her reputation remains intact. A woman will let you do anything with her one night and then pretend to be the perfect wife/mother/girlfriend/chaste girl or whatever the next day at church and think nothing of it. As long as her reputation is safe. While usually this works against men, when you become an attractive man and ascend to the top of the sexual pyramid these dynamics work in your favor. So take responsibility for what happens between you and a woman and then keep in between you two and you two alone and you will have women living out their (and your) wildest fantasies, quicker than you ever thought possible.

How To Go From Dud To Stud

Believe it or not it has nothing to do with having billions, having six pack abs, or having any other false ideals about what women want. You can go from dud to stud instantly by following what is lain out below. The tips lain out below form the foundation of being an attractive man. When these are based on an even greater foundation of embracing your masculinity and being a masculine man then women will be helpless to you. You can go from dud to stud.

While usually when you hear the phrase dud to stud either dangerous pills or overpriced products are hawked. None of that here. What I have below is what I have found to be the absolutely quickest, easiest way to increase your attractiveness to women. These are all what would be considered "outer game" meaning they are active actions you take. Not sure if that's the usual definition of outer game but frankly neither do I care. That's my definition and the one were going with for this chapter.

I would suggest printing this up and running through it before you go out for quite a while. Eventually the words and what to do will become part of you and you no longer will need to read it. But before that time be sure to keep it somewhere convenient so that you can reference it at your own leisure. Remember repetition is the mother of learning. You'll never get everything out of reading something only one time. It must be repeated to have it's full effect and truly become a deep part of you. But without further ado we will begin to dud to stud process.

Eye Contact

Men make eye contact with women. Never be the first to look

away. Show yourself uninhibitedly to women. Let them know that you are not scared. This shows confidence, dominance, and a host of other good features women love. You should practice making eye contact more with everyone, especially good looking women who you are interested in.

Even if a woman doesn't want you she will still respect you for having the balls to look her in her eyes and if anything it will create attraction for you. Even if there wasn't any already there. Looking another person in the eyes requires balls which are one hundred times sexier than a six pack or a large wallet.

Project your thoughts and feelings for her through your eyes. Don't hold back. Look into her eyes unashamedly and completely. Be a man. She wants it and there are very few men who have the guts to do it. Be the guy who is going to take her breath away. And remember never be the first to look away.

Smile

You should always be smiling. It puts you in a good mood as well as releases feel good chemicals throughout your body. People who smile more are going to have more enjoyable lives. When you put yourself in a good mood you are more likely to interact with others and express yourself.

Smiling also shows others that you are social and women will be intrigued when you smile at them. As you should. In addition to look into the eyes of women that you find attractive you should also smile at them. This combined with your eye contact will go far to create or increase a woman's attraction to you.

I should make one caveat here. When I say smile I don't mean a full teeth showing, smile at the camera because I'm a four year old smile. That smile is submissive and weak and will just turn women off. What I mean is more of a smirk. Make sure you're smiling but not a full faced goofy looking one. Smile like a man, not like a boy.

Physical Touch

If there is one thing that turns a woman on more than anything else it is physical touch. Women are more tactile while men are more visual. Many women complain that men don't touch them more. Women want to be touched. Just like men want to see attractive women.

A woman getting touched by a man is like a man seeing an

attractive women take off her clothes. Remember women are more tactile and men are more visual. So you know that feeling you get and how stimulated you are when a smoking hot girl is taking off her clothes for you. Women feel that same way when being touched by a man. Don't be selfish and touch her.

Touch her confidently and with apology. Touch her like a man (it really all comes down to this, being a man). You must get used to touching women and do it often. Touch her on the arm, shoulder, or lower back and progress from there. Don't touch her timidly or you'll come across as a little boy. Touch her like she is already yours.

A note on touching start out light and progress from there. Calibrate your touch, don't just go groping from her like some desperate drunk slob. Calibrate. Passive acceptance of touch means keep escalating. So start out light but all means keep progressing. Slowly but surely you will work her up.

Voice

Many men (especially around good looking women) talk way too fast. They talk like if they don't get out everything they have to say in five seconds they will be interrupted. You need to slow down the rate at which you talk. Talk like a man not like a boy. Meaning don't rush your words take your time with every word. You're not in a hurry.

Speak slowly and enunciate every word. Don't worry if you forget something or there is a pause in the conversation. Only insecure people worry about pauses. They shouldn't even register to you. Just take the conversation in the direction that you want. But make sure to speak slowly and enunciate.

In addition to speaking slowly you should also speak clearly and loudly. You don't have to shout but make sure you are not whispering. Do all this in addition to speaking clearly. So when you speak make sure that each word has enough value, is said clearly, and that it is said slowly. Also having a deeper voice doesn't hurt. Speak from the voice deep in your chest not the one in your nose. All of these thing become habits when you do them enough, never forget that.

Great Attitude

A man has a great attitude towards life, no exceptions. Men do not sit around and whine or mope. Even when the worst is thrown at them they stand strong, resolute, and happy. They laugh with cheer in the face of death. The point is there is no place for anger, hatred, or negativity to weigh you down.

You must cultivate a great attitude. A zest for life and existence. See every day as a blessing because it is. Have a positive attitude towards life. Be optimistic. This doesn't mean to be Pollyanna in your outlook. Simply to be positive. Keep negative things away from you and focus on positive things. Until you entire outlook is reflecting that which you are focusing on. As it inevitably will.

In addition to this have an open vibe. Meaning you are open

to new experiences and people. Women can pick up on this and it draws them to you (among other things). Always be up for an adventure. Have a devil may care attitude. Don't let the things of this world keep you down. Keep your masculine spirit free and wild as it was born to be. A man with his spirit in tact will stand out to all in the best way possible and women absolutely love it. Rise above, don't let this world bring you down.

Always expect a positive outcome, you most often get what you expect. Remember you are the man women love men, they are desperate for you. They want you to approach them, to meet a real man for once in their life. Give them that opportunity. Have confidence in yourself. You're the prize, she's the lucky one.

From Dud To Stud

Be a man. This is what it all fundamentally comes down to. Being a man. However what that means has been severely misconstrued and willfully distorted by our society among other factors. Going from dud to stud is a process of going from boy to man. It doesn't matter your physical age you could still have the mindset of a boy. Few ever truly become fully men. Few go from dud to stud completely.

Be forward and bold. Be a man. You are the active force she is the passive. You are the dominant and she the submissive. This is how it is supposed to be and how she wants it to be. Women love men. Women are waiting for you to make a move. To be the stud they dream of. It doesn't take much to go from dud to stud. Read the above and go out and do them. Go out and go from dud to stud and sweep the women you want off their feet…they're waiting.

Two Of The Most Important Tenets For Understanding Women

There are certain things that are always good to keep in mind when it comes to sleeping with the women you want. Certain tenets of game that once they are firmly cemented in your mind will help your tremendously in developing the love life that you want and desire. The tenets are multiple but the more that you grasp the better off you will be. You can get laid without grasping any of them as getting laid is easy but the more you grasp the easier it becomes.

The basics of game are required knowledge for any man. Every man at some point in his life is going to want to have sex with lots of women and if he never has the ability to he will always be unsatisfied. I'm not saying that a man needs to or even should sleep with a lot of women simply that as a man there is a stage where he will want to know at least know he has the capacity to sleep with the women he wants. Once he does he can generally move on to other stages of his life. However most men never get out of this stage as they never learn game and inter-gender dynamics

Game Tenet #1 – Be Unapologetic About Your Sexual Desire

You know that a key part of being a man is being unapologetic but do you understand how that relates to having sex with the women that you want? It relates in variety of ways but the way that I want you to understand is this. A man should be unapologetic about his sexuality and his sexual desire. A man having a natural desire for a man is considered wrong in our society and men learn to be ashamed of their sexuality. Women who flaunt it are empowered. But be a man desiring a woman and that will get you in trouble.

Learn to be proud of your desire for a woman. Embrace it and show it to others. Don't hide it or be ashamed of it. Both conservative and liberal or however you want to divide people believe that women's sexuality is something that is good while men's is bad. To conservatives men are brutes who prey on pure innocent women and to liberals men are evil who express their sexuality (unless it's perverted) and women are empowered the more sexual they are. Don't listen to either one of them, they both have unhealthy unnatural viewpoints that are not based in nature or logic. Be unapologetic about your sexual desire for women. Show it.

Game Tenet #2 – Be Forward With Your Intentions

There has been a debate on whether it is better to be direct with a woman about wanting her or whether to be indirect. Direct is better. Direct is more masculine and more effective. When you have sexual desire for a woman show that to her. I'm not saying walk up to a woman and say "Hey I want to bang you" although sometimes that works. I mean show that you are relating to her in a sexual way as man to woman. That this is a platonic conversation but one with sexual undertones. Don't be afraid to lose women as the ones you lose when you show your sexual intent were just going to waste your time anyways.

There is an argument that some girls need to be warmed up so if you go direct and scare them away so to speak you won't get them when you could have if you warmed her up first. I understand the logic behind this argument as well as how it can work sometimes but I still would caution you to be direct. Here's why. While it's true that yes you can scare some women off by being forward that you might have otherwise gotten (hence the importance of calibrating and reading women's cues) but for every one that could have been warmed up there are eight that are just wasting your time. Plus it's easier to just go for the ones that are already into it. They will be more receptive and more fun anyways. Be forward with woman about your intentions, don't hide them or try to manipulate.

Summary

So two things to keep in mind when it comes to game. Be unapologetic about your sexual desires for a woman. Women want to be wanted, they desire to be desired. Hiding this from them is just cruel. Of course always calibrate but still show the desire. Don't be ashamed of it or try to hide it. Be unapologetic about what you want from a woman. It is naturally and healthy to desire women, don't be ashamed of it.

The second tenet to keep in mind is to make the interaction a sexual one. Which simply means make it so it isn't a platonic interaction. Show your intentions and desires. Again this doesn't necessary mean "I want to bang you" but rather it's communicated through eye contact, body language, etc. You are relating to her as a man with sexual desires to a woman with sexual needs. Not as two friends, not as two people, but as man to woman. Turn the interaction sexual. You're not talking to her to learn about what she's buying, or her opinions on something, or God forbid something as feminine as what to wear. You talking to her to see if she is sexually worthy of you and will be fun and compatible with you. Be forward with your sexual desires.

Everything You Need To Know To Pass "Shit Tests"

Every man at some point in his relations with women is going to have to deal with shit tests and if he hopes to be successful with many women he is going to have to deal with a lot of them. For those who are wondering "what the hell is a shit test?" let me explain. Shit tests are essential when a woman tests you on something, when she calls you out on something to see how you react. For example you might be talking to her and she says she doesn't date/fuck/whatever short/bald/whatever guys to see if she can break your frame. This is a shit test.

Most men fail shit tests as most men have been trained by the media, overbearing mothers, the government, the school systems, and just about everything else that he is supposed to give in to women. Despite that this goes against the natural order of how nature works. The woman gives into the man not vice versa. This false belief that men should give into women has given many men problems with their relations to women. They get stepped on or a woman loses all attraction for them because the man gives in to them. What I aim to do here is show you how to pass a shit test by asserting your masculinity and making women incredibly attracted to you.

Passing Shit Tests

When a girl is giving you a shit test, she is challenging you. What she is doing is testing your balls to see if you actually have any or to see if you're going to be like ninety nine percent of guys and give in to her (in which case she loses all attraction). She is seeing if you are actually a man or if you are a little boy pretending to be a man. She wants to see your masculinity, that is why she is testing you. To see if there is masculinity there.

While a guy can just look at a woman and see if he is attracted to her it doesn't work that way with women when seeing if a guy is attractive. So a shit test is to see if the guy is actually attractive. Imagine if all women wore burkas a shit test would be the male equivalent of seeing what was under the burka. Is she hot or not. That is what women are trying to see. Is he masculine (and therefore attractive) or is he submissive (and therefore repellent)?

Despite common belief shit tests are not a bad thing. She is trying to see who you are. So when you show her that you are a man and don't give into her. She is going to respond by being even more attracted to. However if you give in to her she is going to lose whatever attraction she had for you in the first place. This works similarly to when you put a woman in her place. If you don't she will lose attraction for you.

Maintain The Frame

To pass a shit test you simply must hold your masculine frame. Maintaining the frame is key in so many things in relations to women. From deciding what kind of relationship you want with them to their overall attraction, love, and desire for you. You as the man should have the stronger frame. Your frame should dominate her frame as the masculine dominates the feminine. Your frame and masculinity should conquer her frame and masculinity. This is how it was meant to be, this is how he wants it, and this is how it works out best for everyone.

Let's break shit tests down even more. Essentially if she say X is Y but you think Z is Y then Z is Y. Or put another way. She says guys who wear boots are lame. You wear boots and you are awesome therefore her statement is false and yours is true. When you hold true to your frame that you are an awesome and attractive guy and don't give in she will give in to it (like she wants to do but she first has to test you to make sure you are genuine). Always keep the frame your awesome and anything that contradicts that frame is B.S., don't give in to her tests and she'll love you for it. She's looking for a guy with masculinity who's frame will dominate hers and be congruent.

Many guys talk big game but then give in at the slightest push. They have no masculinity and women hate this. As far as frame goes remember that your perception is your reality. What you think you create. If you think you are great than you are great. You mold reality (and her frame) to your will (and frame). Bring the girl into your stronger reality. She will submit her weaker reality to your stronger reality and love it and be attracted to you for it.

Summary

Shit tests are how a woman tests to see your masculinity (and therefore attractiveness). Give in and she'll lose all respect and attraction for you. Stand your ground, maintain the frame, and she'll get even more attracted to you. She wants your frame to conquer her frame, your masculinity to conquer her femininity, and eventually for you to conquer her. You are the king and she is the subject, this is how it is supposed to be and this is how women truly deep down want it. It is what fulfills both men and women when they are acting out their natural roles.

Shit tests are battles of the frames in which she is desperately hoping that you are strong enough for your frame to win so that she can submit to you. Don't be like the ninety nine percent of guys who are weak and give in. Be a man and stand strong and as I say the woman will fall at your feet. Remember the frame is you're awesome and you're the man and nothing on this earth or anywhere else will sway you from that. Maintain the frame and pass her tests like a boss by keeping your balls intact. Be the man you were created to be.

3 Mindset Switches To Make That'll Have You Getting Laid 10x As Much

Having lots of sex is a mindset. To get laid a lot you have to have the right beliefs. I know that goes against much of what you have heard but it is the truth. Looks, money, fame and such while attractive women are not the way to go about having the sex life that you want. There are ways that are much easier and exponentially more effective. Take one man who all the looks, fame, money, or whatever else society has led you to believe women want and put him up against a man who has the right mindset in regards to bedding lots of women and the man with the right mindset is going to come out on top every time.

I'm not denying that women don't like looks, money, or fame. Looks are nice to make their girlfriends jealous, money is good to take advantage of, and fame is nice to again make her girlfriends jealous. However there are much more effective ways. For example being a dominant masculine man turns women on viscerally. Enough that she'll forget about her good looking, rich, famous boyfriend or husband. And no I'm not kidding. If you want to be a good target then by all means pursue looks, money, and fame to the exclusion of developing yourself as man. However if you'd rather be the man women want rather than use then you have to go about it a different way. And your mindset is the start.

Switch #1 – The Abundance Mindset

The first thing that you have to realize is that women are incredibly plentiful. Women are everywhere. No matter how sexy/awesome/whatever the girl you are with is there is always one better and younger. Like I said in The Primer "Most women are interchangeable and all women are replaceable.", women are an abundant resource.

Remember having an abundance mindset is an essential part of all aspects of your life, women are not exception. Women are not rare but bountiful. You can always get a newer better one.

Many guys get caught up in one girl on in a few select girls. They fail to see the opportunity all around them. Every day new beautiful women come of age and this cycle is not stopping. Women are abundant. Never focus on a woman (or a few women) to the exclusion of all women. There are more beautiful women in the world than you could ever hope to sleep with. Like an all you can eat buffet. Even if you wanted to eat it all you couldn't. The same holds true with women. They are an abundant, you might as well worry about the ocean running out of water than worrying about not finding a better/great/sexy woman.

Switch #2 – Women Are Easy

I don't say this as a derogatory term but simply as fact. While men are often given the easy label (because they are) the truth is women are also easy just one they hide it and two there has to be certain stipulations. Meet those stipulations and it's game on. Women are easy granted that you are the right man. Sure if you are a wimp with no game no women aren't going to be easy for you. They'll put you in the friend zone and hope one day you get rich or famous or good looking enough so they can live off you while banging their deadbeat ex-boyfriend.

Women are easy. Get this in your mind. Women will have sex with the right man within five minutes of meeting him if things are right. Only suckers think they have to go on dates with women or spend a certain amount of time with them before they can have sex. Women will have sex with a guy they just met if he turns her on. This holds true for all types of women not just women most would label "easy". Remember all women are easy if you are a man. Get this in your head as society programs you to believe women are hard when in fact they are just playing hard. That's why it's called playing hard to get not being hard to get.

Switch #3 – Women Love Sex

This also goes against what society and the majority of men

would have you believe. They say women only want money or flowers but they hate sex. When hate to break it to them but women only want money and flowers from men who have nothing else to offer. They want sex from real men and are most likely getting sex from real men why you empty your wallet or affection to them. Women love sex with real dominant men. Look at how well *50 Shades of Grey* has sold.

Women love sex. Of course that's only with the right men. This is something that most men will have to work to get into their heads. Women are sexual creatures. They all have sexual thoughts, feelings, and desires often raunchy and more hardcore than the average man would expect. Of course they do a great job of hiding this from the average guy as they are afraid of being judged for it. Women have many of the same feelings as guys its just that women hide and mask things much more than men do and are much less likely to admit things that have the potential to tarnish their reputation. Remember a woman will do anything so long as her reputation remains intact.

Summary

To get laid a lot you have to have the right beliefs and the right mindset. The three beliefs above go against much of your social programming (which has misled you). If this is your first exposure to these ideas it may take some time to sink in but keep them in your mind and trust me they will sink in. Go out and test these ideas and when you find them to be true they will sink in even deeper. Instead of pursing money, looks, and fame to be a good target instead pursue the right mindset and be a man.

Then you will be the man women desire instead of the man women use. Others will wonder how and why you get laid so much but you will know. It is because you have the right mindset and therefore the right beliefs regarding women and sex. You see everything stems from your mindset. Have the right beliefs and your life lines up accordingly. Have the right beliefs regarding money and you will get rich and so on and so forth. All is mindset, including making sure you get laid a lot.

2 Things That Turn Women On Like Crazy

Ask most men or God forbid
women what makes women/them
hot and bothered and you'll get a
variety of answers. Ninety nine
percent of which are completely ass
backwards wrong. For starts the
vast majority of men aren't very
successful with women. The vast
majority of men aren't having the
sex they want with the women they
want. If they are having sex at all
it's with whatever woman that they
settled for as they believed (as
society wants them to) that sex is

something that women give to men and that men are "lucky" to get it.

These men are men at the bottom of the sexual pyramid, the beta or sometimes even omega males. Women are no better and often worse. Ask them what gets women hot and bothered and they will tell you the complete opposite of what gets them hot and bothered. Whether this is done purposely or women are just that oblivious (my money's on the latter) matters little. Listening to a woman's advice on women is a guaranteed way to never get laid.

For men who want to actually have success with women their best bet is going against what society says will get them women and what women say will get them women. Namely going against be the nice guy, do everything she wants, lavish her with praise, money, and devotion, etc. Instead be a man and the women will fall at your feet. Part of being a man is doing the two things listed below.

Not Taking Their Shit

Women have been conditioned by society and the media that men are going to take their shit. That they can say and do whatever they want and that men should sit there with a smile and take it. Never mind that it turns them off like a hairy obese women turns off a man but women are much more prone to going alone with society (or anyone's) B.S. then men are. When you don't take crap from a woman not only is she going to be shocked in a good way but also turned on like never before. Imagine if you walked up a woman in bent over like an old lady in a hooded robe only for her to stand up turn around discard to robe and be a smoking hot twenty year old blonde with a 1.6 hip to waist ratio. That's what happens to women when you don't take their shit.

Now don't get me wrong at first they will test you as they can't believe what they've found. Imagine if you woke up one morning to a pile of gold bricks by your bed. You'd be skeptical or the very least confused. Before telling your boss to shove it you'd test out that gold and make sure it was real. Same with women when they find a man that actually causes attraction in them and a lot of it. They're so used to lame placating girly males (including good looking and rich men) who they want to have some sort of feelings for (other than disgust) but they can't. Then you come along and turn them on like a dying fire getting gasoline poured onto it. All from something as simple as not taking their shit.

Calling Them Out On Their Shit

Not taking their shit will wow them enough, if you add it into calling them out on their shit and they will love you for eternity. You see women often act bratty and out of hand because they want to see if there is a man who is actually a man out there and will call them out on it. They want a man who will put them in their place. I've had women specifically try me just because they knew that I wouldn't tolerate it and would say something. I would call them out on it and they loved it.

Women know they are full of shit. If anything get frustrated that men don't know this. Now no woman is ever going to come out and say "I and all women are full of shit" just like no woman is ever going to come out and say "Hey me and the rest of women prefer assholes who hump and dump us over nice guys who wine and dine us". It just isn't going to happen. It'd kill the fun. Just like it doesn't count if a woman has to tell a man to be dominate, she just wants him to get it. If she had to tell him, by nature of her telling him to be dominant he wouldn't be dominant because he'd just be doing what she said to do. Not doing something organically. Women are desperate for real men. They want you to be a man and call them out on their shit, more than you want them to stop acting a certain way. Do yourselves both a favor and call them out.

Summary

Now a caveat is this all must be done from a place of simply doing it because you want to. What I mean is, if a woman annoys you, you don't lash out emotionally at her like a little boy. You stay unemotional like a rock and simply state facts. You don't give in to her hysterics or annoying behavior or whatever, you maintain the frame. And you don't get all whiny and complain either. Men never whine or complain, they solve problems and get shit done. Simply call her out and don't take shit.

Do these two things and you will be catapulted into the top echelon of men. Women will want you and men will respect you. Which are two things that naturally happen when you embrace your masculinity and reclaim your balls. You will be a man among boys. A king among paupers. You will stand out in this world like a light in the middle of the darkness. So remember don't take women's shit and call them out on their shit. They'll thank you for it (often with sex) and more importantly you will be fulfilling your role as a man by embracing your masculinity.

How To Get A Woman Addicted To You

There are men who have trouble getting a date with women and then there are men who have to beat women off with a stick. While the vast majority of men fall in the former category those men who can get women addicted to them fall into the latter category. The men in the latter category reside near or at the top of the sexual pyramid with women in the middle and then the vast majority of men at the bottom settling for whatever scraps (if any) are thrown their way. This is no way to live. Luckily you can change where you reside on the pyramid and go from the bottom echelons to the very top.

For men who have embraced their masculinity and are men, they have a hard time keeping women away from them. They will have women respond strongly to them wherever they go because women naturally respond strongly to masculinity. They respond strongly to masculinity in societies where masculinity is encouraged and the majority of the population has at least a modicum of masculinity, so in a feminized cancerous society such as our own women are going to respond like crack fiends to men who are masculine. The process of getting a woman addicted to you is relatively simply, just follow what is lain out below. The trick is keeping them off.

Dominate Them

Women love to be dominated by a strong man. They may not admit it but it's the truth. Masculine dominance is to women what a round perky ass is to a guy. A giant turn on. A guy could say till he was blue in the face that he doesn't care if a woman has a nice ass as far as attraction goes but he'd be full of shit. It isn't a choice, it's biological. And as I have said biology trumps societal shaming and any ideology.

Tell women what to do and how you want it done. Have standards that they must meet. Make them perform for you in some way, shape, or form. Don't demand them around like a domineering slave master. Dominance is not barking orders from a place of insecurity, dominance comes from a place of security and is the opposite to domineering. Let women know what you want. If you want them to do something for you, make them. Not angry and fighting but simply by stating the fact if they want to stick around they have to meet certain standards and qualifications.

You're not making them jump through hopes as in a "Ha I'll show her" way. Remember this comes from a place of security and appreciation for the feminine. Not from a place of insecurity and hate. These are simply your standards and she can either meet them and perform or get out. Again not in a hateful way just in a matter of factly way. Women want to perform for you. They want to please you. Show them what does and then let them do so. They'll enjoy every minute of it.

Maintain The Frame

This is key to so much with women and life. As a man you cannot show signs of weakness, or put more accurately you cannot be weak. Weakness has not part in a man's life. Men and women both has disdain for a weak man. A man who plays the victim will always be hated as men are not victims but rather warriors and creators. When something goes wrong in a man's life he doesn't pout and whine. He sarges out and fixes it, he does something about it. Whining and complaining are never an option in a man's life. Nor are bitterness and hatred.

When a man makes a decision or comes to a conclusion he sticks with it. Even if his women or all women are against him he keeps his conclusion and thoughts. A man doesn't change for others regardless of who they are. He doesn't let others shame and control him but rather goes his own way and follows his own path. He is immune to the opinions of others. This doesn't mean he never listens simply that when he makes a decision he sticks with it. He isn't unstable but rather firm and unmoving in his convictions.

A woman will test a man's strength to make sure that he is in fact a man and the what she sees is the real deal. When the man maintains the frame and doesn't change or give in. A woman will know he is the real deal and get even more turned on by him. She will want him more and more as long as he maintains the frame and doesn't budge for her. Or anyone else for that matter. He is a rock that the winds of society and women simply bounce off of. He moves when he wants to move, he will not be moved by others.

Screw Her Good

Good sex equals dominant sex. Again women and others may say otherwise but it doesn't change the truth of the matter. I'll say it again good sex equals dominant sex. Dominate your woman in the bedroom. Tie her up, spank her, make her call you daddy, choke her, and she will soar to heights of ecstasy that she didn't know was possible. It cannot be said enough good sex equals dominant sex.

Romance novels are to women what porn is to men. Trust me if you opened up your average romance novel you're not going to be reading about how the billionaire, vampire, biker, or whatever was lovingly caressing the heroine. No you are going to read about how the heroine was being banged off the wall in wild throes of passion and being used as the male's sexual gratification tool more than anything. That is what equals hot sex. Not tender loving. It's not secret why *50 Shades of Grey* has sold over 100 million copies in record time.

Dominate her in the sack and she will be at your beck and call. Literally she could be on a date with a guy, you could text her, she will leave the date come over screw your brains out knowing she is going to be kicked out once the orgasms are over. But she won't care because of what you're doing to her. Make her cum from your manly dominance and you will be a diamond among coal. A man among boys. A fresh prepared organic steak among piles of dog shit. You'll stand out in her mind above all others and she will be addicted to you.

Summary

Getting women addicted to you is relatively simple. While lame ass PUAs go out and get rejected by girls even the pros only getting laid in one of out one hundred approaches (and no I'm not making that up). Real masculine men go out and have women just about throw themselves at them. They want to be taken and ravished by a real man, not some little boy with his scripts and techniques but a real man. Be a man and the women will fall at your feet, every time.

So if you want a woman to come back anytime you want her to. To be at your beck and call remember to do these three things. Dominate her. Make her do things for you and have standards she has to meet. Make her grow her hair out if it's too short, make her wear heels when she's out with you, make her start a workout routine of your choosing. Not from a place of being domineering but from a place of security and dominance.

Maintain the frame, don't give in to her or others. Show no weakness and always be the man. Dominate her in the bedroom. Get rough with her and she will love you for it. Allow her to be the submissive fuck doll as she has always fantasized about doing. Do these things and she will do whatever you want whenever you want.

Why You Should Always Go For It With Women

You want to know why many guys don't have the sex lives that they want? Sure not having game, being more feminine than they should, worshiping women, and stuff like that plays a part. But ultimately it comes down to this one simple thing. They never go for it, they never approach a woman and show her that they have an interest in her. Despite false popular psychologies belief that women are good readers of people (hint: they aren't) and automatically know when a guy wants them the truth is women are as oblivious as most men. And if a woman doesn't know you're interested she isn't going to show you she is interested and that's even if she is. Women don't want to make the first move it makes them too vulnerable, that is the man's job.

Let me ask you something when you go out to a bar or a place with many women and you are single and don't have a rotating harem of women, how many women do you talk to and interact with? Hell how many do you make eye contact with or smile at? One, two, or if you're like most men zero. How are you supposed to have the sex life you want if you never show your interest in a woman? You won't. That's like expecting to win or even place in a race without ever getting off the couch. Even the worst runner in the world who actually takes action will be ahead of the great runner who never gets off the couch. You have to play then game to win, life is not a spectator sport, and neither is having the relations you want with the opposite sex.

Don't Be Coy

Unfortunately between social conditioning and bad "pickup"

advice men have been told that its good to hide their interest from a woman and to never let her know that you have any desire for her. This comes from insecure men who confess their love and everlasting desire for a woman from the moment they meet her. They over do it and plus they don't really feel those things and if they do then they have to work on their manhood and priorities before anything else. So naturally the advice was to do the opposite of that, never show your interest in a woman. That's the problem with a lot of "pickup" advice, it comes from insecure nerds and is what worked for them but when done by a normal or especially an attractive man doesn't make much sense.

If you're an attractive man and never show women interest, you're not going to get laid a lot. Because you are attractive you are going to intimidate women who already don't want to make the first move. When you show your interest and desire for her however it allows her to express hers, plus she'll get shocked/flattered/turned on like crazy that an attractive masculine man is showing interest in her. The aloof never show a woman any interest stuff is mostly crap when it comes to most situations. Obviously this doesn't mean

supplicate and kiss her feet, be a
man but also show your manly
desires. Don't be coy, show her
how you feel.

Insecurity

But won't that make me beta?
I heard that if you ever tell a
woman anything positive she
cheats on you and runs off with a
guy who treats her like crap. Again
this is advice that came from weak
burned men who were getting to
the next level. They went from total
weak wimps to jerks, which
admittedly is an improvement but
not the final stage of the
evolution. Have a backbone and
show your interest and you won't

have to worry about this. This reminds me of men who say never to smile to women as it is a sign of submissiveness. What they mean is some dumb little boy "smile for mommy" smile which makes them look like children, a key tenet of game is smiling like a man at women.

So a lot of red pill or "pickup" advice comes from men or more accurately boys/males who were insecure and needy so adopted traits of the jerk and lo and behold women responded better. Because these men were actually acting more like men. Honestly treating a women like crap while having some balls will get you more women than worshiping women ever will but that is not the final or most effective stage by a long shot.

Alphas, Jerks, And Nice Guys

I may eventually do a post on my site just on this topic but essentially what happens with much "pickup" advice is that they are beta men. Weak, women worshiping, and balless who get burned by women time and time again so adopt traits that are opposite of them. They adopt the traits of a jerk. So they end up hating women (which is never the answer), disregarding them, and treating them like dirt which admittedly is a step in the right direction. But they are still living for women and are still insecure and will suffer for that. Here in this book I do what's best for men not women. And if being the jerk was best for men, that's what I would advocate but it's not being the alpha is. Now many think the alpha is a nicer version of the jerk, a step back towards beta but this is false.

The alpha is masculine and more masculine than the jerk as he doesn't have insecurity issues or hate. He lives for himself and himself alone. He is the one that can successfully have a harem of young college girls, date a few beautiful models, or have a happy successful marriage with a healthy family. Like I said in The Primer the alpha is a man, fully and whole. He has the capacity to have any type of relationship with the majority of women he wants. He doesn't have to have meaningless sex with low self-esteem girls who later accuse him or rape or revel in his abuse like the jerk. Rather he can have sex with lots of beautiful normal women or have one wife who loves and worships him. The alpha is a man. Be an alpha, the jerk is a weak watered down version of him. The beta even worse. The jerk is a step in the right direction but it's still weak and insecure.

Summary

So go for it. You'll be a step above you aloof jerk friends, you'll have better game than them, be more of a man than them, and have sex with hotter and healthier women than them. Women are not the enemy. Your own weakness is the enemy. When you develop yourself you'll naturally screen out bad women and weak men. Instead of constantly contesting with them because you are on the same level as them. Bitterness, insecurity, and weakness are not traits of a man.

They are traits of a weak boy or a woman.

They have no place in a man's life. When you see a woman you want always go for it. Show your interest in her. Make it clear that you want her. Be bold and forward and ballsy. Be a man…and the women will fall at your feet. Be straightforward about what you want from a woman, don't play the coy little boy, be the confident forward man. Trust me not only is it the best for attracting women, more importantly it's best for your life and your manhood. So ditch the beta mindset but don't get stuck in

the jerks but evolve to the man's.
And always go for it.

How To Create Sexual Tension With A Woman

One of the most important things to have in turning women on and having lots of sex is the understanding of how to create sexual tension between you and a woman. Being able to create and escalate sexual tension with a woman is paramount in sleeping with women. Sexual tension is exactly what it sounds like that buildup of sexual desire and energy that get released during sex. Men don't need it as much as woman as men can see a woman with a nice body and instantly get turned on while women need to be worked up. Of course this process of working up can be done very quickly with a guy who knows what he is doing.

There are many different ways to create sexual tension, some more effective than others. What I am going to do here is lay out the most effective ways to create and build sexual tension with a woman. This is not a complicated process and is in fact a natural one. Remember sex and sexual relations are not complicated or hard, they are natural and once you get in touch with your natural masculinity come very easily. But first you must actively work against your social programming for it to come naturally. The first step is to be aware of what causes sexual tension and how to use it.

Eye Contact & Smile

Making eye contact and smiling at a woman is a very effective way of generating sexual tension. Of course it must be done in the right way. Have a goofy boy smile is not going to create sexual tension while having a man's smile is. You know when a kid smiles teeth showing and like his cheeks are going to swallow his eyes? That's not exactly the smile we are

going for. What we want is a smirk.
You can still smile fully just keep
in mind you're not doing a cheesy
smile for the family portrait rather a
masculine smile to a woman.

Eye contact is incredibly
powerful. In business, in life, in
relations of any kind, and
especially in sexual relations with
women. When you look a woman
in the eyes unashamedly and
confidently (especially with a smirk
on your face) she is going to
respond to this in a good way.
There will be sexual tension
created between you two. You
should try making eye contact with
every woman you meet and with

men in business settings. Only in business settings as locking eyes with a man in public is a sigh of dominance which may cause a fight. Which could also be one reason while women respond so strongly to it.

Touch

When I say touch I don't mean full on groping. No I mean little touches here and there, then gradually progress. A touch on the lower back, arm, or shoulder. Moving a piece of her hair out of the way or just anything really. A lingering touch builds even more tension. That thing with touch it you want to calibrate it and escalate slowly at first. As you progress you will naturally know how and when to touch but for starters do it lightly and then work from there. Women love being touched, especially by a confident masculine man.

I would say touch is the potential strongest builder of sexual tension. If you could choose just one thing to give you the most bang for your buck this would be it. However utilize all methods as they all work and work even better together. So start off touching women lightly and here and there then progress once you learn to calibrate and read. When it doubt, always go for it. If you are going to mess up, mess up on the side of aggression rather than timidity. Timidity has no place in a man's life.

Flirting/Teasing

This works incredibly well with certain girls. While some girls (especially more traditional/feminine ones in my experience) respond better to a masculine direct approach many women (especially masculinized Western women) respond better to getting their chops busted and being teased. While both touch, making eye contact, and smiling can all be considered flirting what I mean here is verbal flirting. Which is the least effective of all the methods yet still works especially for girls who play hard to get or are into playing games.

For girls who want to play games teasing and giving them backhanded compliments is the way to go. Girls who respond to this tend to respond strongly to this. Girls who like to tease and as I said play hard to get respond real well to this. Works well with girls who think their better than everyone as well. Popping their bubble is going to throw them and throw them in a good way. I prefer girls who don't play games but its always good to know how to bang a variety. Even if you prefer deer sometimes it's good to know how to hunt other animals as well.

Sexual Tension

One thing to keep in mind with all this is that as a man you should always be relating to women as a man. Not as a asexual person but as a man. She is a woman and you are a man. Meaning there are dynamics there that will always be in place. Never relate to a woman of any kind as anything other than a man. Especially women that you want to have sexual relations with. So many men in today's world neuter themselves to get close to women not realizing how that will backfire on them. As they will be seen as a gelded plaything and not as a man.

All of the above is predicated on you being a man and relating to women as a man. You were created to be a man and when you neuter yourself for whatever reason you are spitting in the face of God and yourself. Have respect for yourself and always be a man.
Remember there is no competition for masculine men and there is no honor for feminine men. Embrace and be who you were created to be, fully and completely a man.

A Pillar Of Good Game That Is Rarely Mentioned

You've probably heard at some point in your life how important your attitude is. How attitude is the number one determining factor in where you end up, how attitude is the one thing you have control over, how life is ten percent what happens to you and ninety percent how you deal with it. I am in agreement with all the above and think that if anything these phrases understate the importance of your attitude.

Your attitude is an essential part of having a sex life filled with beautiful women. That's right your attitude or mood matters just as much in having sex with women as it does with getting a promotion, getting closer in a relationship, or just having an overall much better life.

The Importance Of Your Mood

Your mood matters tremendously in relating to women. Women are much more sensitive to a man's mood than men are to women's mood. Women are emotional creatures and live in a world of emotions. When you are in a bad mood even if you are attractive and alpha you are still going to prevent women from opening up to you. Likewise when you are in a good mood you are naturally going to draw women to you who also want to be in a good mood.

Remember men are the actors women are the reactors. Of course being in a good mood in and of itself isn't enough. You also have to follow the basics of being a man and game. Otherwise you'll have women who want to be around you but only to get the good emotional feelings from you, you'll end up being the "gay best friend" type.

Which I'm quite certain no one reading this wants.

Emotions Transfer

The emotions you have (especially if you are a strong man) transfer to those around you. If you are in a good mood and having a good time a woman can sense this and wants to be a part of this. This is key to picking up women at clubs and bars. Get in a good mood and your results are going to shoot up tenfold. You could have great game and be attractive but if you are in a low energy bad mood you're going to be shooting yourself in the foot every time you go out.

You mood matters greatly.
Which is why I recommend
that when you go out you focus on
yourself and on having a good
time. That way your mood is going
to automatically transfer to those
around you which is naturally
going to draw women into your
frame. The frame of having a good
time. Combine that with being
masculine and having decent game
and your not going to have to
worry about going home alone
again.

Girls Just Want To Have Fun

Always remember this.
Women are all addicted. They are
all addicted to good emotions and

they are going to go wherever they can get their fix. Technically their addicted to emotions bad or good but good is going to win out in the end. Women are emotional creatures living in emotional worlds. Hence the effectiveness of things like emotional spiking and teasing.

Women are reactive by nature they are going to react to the dominant emotion that you are feeling. They are going to give you space if you are angry, brooding, or in a negative mood. Likewise they are going to be drawn towards a guy who is laughing, smiling, and having a good time.

Summary

Next time you are going out be sure to get in a good mood before doing so. It might help to have a routine that you do every time or maybe it'll help to have a good wingman you can rely on to get you in state. Point is, do what you have to do to get the good emotions flowing. If that means having a drink then have a drink. If it means laughing then laugh. As a matter of fact if you don't have a wingman smiling and laughing may be the best way to get you in state. You may feel a little weird smiling and laughing at nothing but eventually the emotions will catch on and it'll make for a much better night out.

The Roots Of Sexual Attraction

You've probably heard the phrase "attraction isn't a choice" it rings true but have you ever stopped to think about why this is? Why isn't attraction a choice? Why can a man be a giant asshole who all women are "supposed" to hate get laid left and right and yet the politically correct male that does everything society tells him to ends up with his hand night after night? This is because attraction is based in biology, not ideology. And as we all know biology always, always, always trumps ideology.

Hence it makes sense that the roots of sexual attraction are going to be based on human biology. The same biology humans were created with and that the last man will have when it all ends. This biology can be resisted but it cannot be overridden and males have a much higher capacity to resist their biology then women who are all essentially slaves to it. Then again most males are as well.

The Roots Of Sexual Attraction

So what is the root of sexual attraction between men and women. We know that things like dominance, taking charge, and passing shit tests all turn a woman on yet why exactly is this? What is the underlying factor at play here? Is it strength? In a sense yes yet it isn't strength in and of itself. Alright what about dominance, we're getting closer but even dominance in and of itself isn't the root. We can look at a bunch of different factors but still come up short. Only by looking at the root can we truly grasp what attraction is and what causes it.

The root cause of attraction for women is masculinity and the root cause of attraction for men is femininity. Not what society says is masculine and feminine which can be completely misconstrued and is usually done for propaganda and social engineering purposes more than anything. But rather what our biology says is masculine and feminine, which never has changed and never will change. What made Bo the caveman attracted to Sally the cave girl will make Don the advertising exec attracted to Kelly his secretary and vice versa.

Expressions

The reason that dominance, taking charge, and passing shit tests all hit a woman's button is because they are all expressions of masculinity. It's the same with teasing or giving a woman a backhanded compliment it expresses confidence and other traits that all are expressions of masculinity. Likewise when a woman is smiling, bubbly, submissive, kind, loving, and has 36-24-36 figure (with that being the most important factor) she is going to be incredibly attractive to men because of how highly she expresses her femininity.

The higher you express your masculinity the more attractive you are to women and the higher a woman expresses her femininity the more attractive she will be to men. However some misinterpret this polarity and fall into some errors. One is that men and women both have a feminine and masculine nature in them. This is not true. Males can "ape" feminine behavior and females can "ape" masculine behavior but just like the ape "apeing" a human doesn't make him one a male or female aping the behavior of the other sex doesn't give him or her that energy.

Reality

Some think that "Well masculine women will be attracted to feminine men and vice versa" but they are wrong and their thinking patterns have been polluted by society (just like the "apeing" example above). "Masculine" females are masculine because there is not masculinity around them that they can submit to. Feminine males are just broken and need to be fixed by the men around them. Masculine females are broken to but simply need to interact with a masculine man to quickly resume their natural role.

For example I've seen bitchy "masculine" women turn into submissive (and often horny) lambs around me and other men like me much to the shock of their beta boyfriends. Every man wants a feminine woman and every woman wants a masculine man. Even lesbians want men. This basic truths are taboo in our society. But it doesn't matter. There is no need to fight the useless fight against society. Rather accept these truths and learn from them. Build the life you want and let society crumble in its lies.

Summary

The truth will set you free. The root of sexual attraction is the polarity between the masculine and the feminine that is rooted in our biology not what society says. There is no such thing as femininity in males or masculinity in females they can only "ape" one another and when they do it makes them repulsive in every way. "Masculine" females are simply females who haven't been exposed to real masculinity and "feminine" males suffer from corrupted ways of thinking and need to be set straight if they are to not suffer through life. Always remember biology trumps ideology.

Three Frames That Create Massive Amounts Of Attraction In Women

Women can sense a man's power, meaning they can sense his innate dominance and masculinity. They can sense if he has balls and what kind of man that he is. I'm not saying they can sense it to an incredible degree but they can tell if a guy is the kind of guy who would put them in their place like they want or let them walk all over them. And despite what many believe it has little to do with how muscular a guy is or how well he's dressed or the best how rich he is. There are plenty of muscular, well dressed, rich males who get used and abused by women every day.

This is about something much deeper. An inner power and a mindset that permeates everything that a masculine man does. Masculine men interact with women in a number of different ways, they interact with them using certain "frames" if you will. When a women interacts with a man and he is operating from one of these frames she knows that she is in the presence of a strong masculine man and responds accordingly. When you interact with women you should (at least the majority of the time) be operating from one of the following three frames.

Frame #1 – Challenging

You know the males that go along with everything that a woman says? The "yes dear" type of males who walk around with their balls in their significant other's (or their mother's) purse. Yeah being one of those males is guaranteed way to repel women like crazy and never get laid. Women thrive on stimulation and always agreeing and being a doormat is a great way to never stir up anything in a woman (other than disgust).

Confident men have no problem challenging women they meet. Sometimes because what the woman is saying is stupid and she has never been put in her place and other times because he enjoys getting a reaction out of her. You should have no problem ever challenging a woman on anything or calling them out. Many times women are just waiting for a man to call them out. They desperately want a strong man they can submit too.

Frame #2 – Commanding

Do you make demands of your women? Do you tell them what to do and when you want it done? If not you need to start. Commanding is another frame that causes lots of attraction in women. Women want to be told what to do by strong men and love serving strong men. A man who isn't afraid to tell a woman what he wants done and have a woman do things for him is a man who is going to get lots of female attention and more importantly female desire.

When you meet a woman for the first time who ends up in the lead? It should always be you. Women have an innate need and desire to serve but the issue is they cannot serve what they don't respect. That is why you have weak males who would cringe/laugh nervously at a chapter like this because they would say their women would never go for it. And they're right their women would never go for it…with them but would more than happily go for it with a strong man.

Frame #3 – Teasing

This is the frame where you treat all women like silly little girls where you don't really take anything they say seriously and tease them. Even at full maturity women are still essentially little girls at heart. One popular phrase is to see women as "the most responsible teenager in the house" that's being a little generous with the majority of women but you get the point. Men who take everything a woman says with the same seriousness and care as if a man said it are fools. This isn't to say women never say something of worth because they do.

Women love to be teased. Women know deep down that they need to be lead and that what they say should always be taken with a grain of salt (sometimes more like a heaping spoonful) and respect men who know this. You're the leader and she's the silly little girl. You'll know you're doing it right when a woman tell you how much she "hates you" while giggling uncontrollably and grabbing your arm.

Summary

So there you have it the three frames that masculine men take when they interact with women. They are either challenging a woman calling her out and busting her chops. Commanding a woman telling her what to do and making it know they are the master. Or teasing a woman making her feel like the little girl she knows she is and not taking her seriously. Make sure that your interactions with women take on one of the three above and rest assured once you become a fully masculine man that this will all come naturally, though it will require practice if you're not already there. Just keep at it you'll get there eventually.

Why Sleeping With Women Should Never Be Your #1 Priority

Look all men want to sleep with many beautiful women at some point in their life. To deny this is to lie to yourself. However many males make the mistake of making this their number one focus. Sleeping with lots of women. Now I am not denying that sleeping with women or eventually a woman isn't an important part of a man's life because it is and to deny it would be stupid. Women are going to be a large part of a man's life. Hence why I write so much about attraction, however it is a mistake to make women/a woman/sleeping with women your number one priority for a variety of reasons.

There are literally thousands of reasons why this will not work. What I am going to point out here is why this is foolish even if your only goal is to sleep with a lot of women. That's right even if all you want to do is bang a lot of women making sleeping with lots of women your number one priority is going to backfire on you. I'm not saying it can't be up there because there are times in your life when it will be but it can never be number one. Again even if all you want to do is bang lots of women. So without further ado let's get started.

It Hampers You More Than Anything

Even if all you want to do is bang a lot of women making it your number one priority is going to hamper you more than anything. Women shouldn't be your number one priority. Becoming a man (which will in and of itself attract women, something PUAs nerds never figured out) should be your number one priority. When you make women your number one priority (which they don't even want to be) you are actually repelling them. Especially if you are already not getting laid as much as you want to. Making women your number one priority is just going to exacerbate this problem even more.

Men who make sleeping with women their number one priority generally don't have a lot going for them which makes sleeping with lots of women even harder. Focusing on yourself is going to give you a much higher ROI than focusing on the women that you want to sleep with. It's much better to attract than try to pursue when you have nothing going for you in the first place or even if you have very little going for you. Or really ever though there is a time when you will have to do some pursuing of your own (but it won't be your number one priority).

A Lesson From The PUAs

By lesson I mean how not to do something and an example of the complete wrong way to do it. So many PUAs make sleeping with women their number one priority (even over being masculine or being an attractive dominant masculine man women will naturally be drawn to). Let's look at the closing rates of some of the top PUAs. I'm not going to name names or anything but these are some statistics I've seen and shows how completely ineffectual their methods of putting sleeping with women first are.

One PUA talked about approaching two thousand women and having ten (as in 10, one zero) women sleep with him. I know lame guys in high school who did better than that. Another talked about approaching women using "day game" and approached eight hundred women and slept with sixteen. A little better but still a complete loser. And third one who approached one hundred women and slept with one. And these are the supposed "pros" (go ahead laugh along with me). These males obviously don't value their most precious resource.

Now that should show how completely ineffectual making sleeping with women your number one priority is. I know guys who haven't approached one hundred women in their life yet have banged seventy or so women. Because they don't make sleeping with women their number one priority. Think how ridiculous this is. Who values their time so little? To me it seems it take a special kind of loser to be a PUA. Not that everyone who falls under the PUA term is a loser because it quite far reaching but you get my point.

Focus On Being An Attractive Man

Look I don't even want you to focus on working out or your style much less sleeping with women. That is not where you focus should go. Instead focus on being an dominant masculine attractive man and you'll sleep with nine out of ten women that you want. Spend your time in developing yourself. Learn sales, how to fight, and how to be a man. That should be your number one priority. Sleeping with women never should be, women in general never should be. It does nothing but harm you. That is why the PUA mentality fucks guys up so much it is the completely wrong mentality to have. It puts the cart before the horse for starters and messes up a man's priorities badly. Again not everything that is lumped under PUA is bad but the general theme of PUA certainly is.

Remember even if you are that stage of your life when what you want most is bang a lot of women, making their your number one priority is still going to backfire on you. Focus on yourself and your life. Banging women can be up there in your priorities but never number one. That's how an attractive man does it, stay away from the weirdo PUA losers and rather be a man. Remember once you become a man the women will fall at your feet.

3 Politically Incorrect Truths About Women

Women are interesting creatures. Much has been devoted to understanding them in order to have them occupy the correct part of your life. Like I said in The Primer women can either be one of the greatest sources of pleasure and fun in your life or one of the greatest sources of pain and frustration in your life. All depending on whether you understand them and their nature or not.

Men who understand women and their nature know how to treat women. They know not to take shit from them and that what they say they want and what they actually want are usually two completely different things, often opposites in fact. They also understand how women view men and understand things like hypergamy and the rationalization hamster. These men understand the truth about women and therefore are able to relate to them successfully and properly. As man to woman.

Yet as every good scholar knows you can always expand your knowledge and by doing so produce better results and a more right form of living. Put another way knowledge is power. And you can never have enough of either. Here are some more truths to mull over in your pursuit of living a life of your dreams and reclaiming your freedom.

A Woman's Disdain For Nice Guys

What repulses women? Men, being men are naturally going to say ugly guys as men ugly women are what repulses us. But it is not so simple. Women attraction unlike men's is not based on looks but rather other factors such as dominance. Put simply when it comes to women, look don't matter that much and they matter far less than you have been led to think. It's funny you'll see guys spend hours at the gym and when asked they give you reason x or y but the reality is they train to look good for women, thinking looking better will net them more women as a woman who improves her looks will net her more men. But it doesn't work that way for men and working for aesthetics and aesthetics only is quite a feminine pursuit. How long before men start putting on makeup in an effort to look better in an attempt to attract more women?

Anyways no it is not ugly men who repulse women rather is it submissive nice guys that repulse women, at least sexually. Don't get me wrong women love taking advantage of these type of men whether for monetary purposes or to use them as emotional tampons but sexually they are repulsed by them. Women have an innate disdain for weak men and many times aren't afraid to show it. It is biologically built into women as a survival mechanism and still applies today just as much as it did roaming the jungles of prehistoric times.

A Woman's Desire For Bad Boys

Like a woman is naturally repulsed by a nice guy, they are naturally attracted (aka get wet for) bad boys. Now bad boys means different things to different people but overall gives the idea of a guy who could care less about the woman, uses her for sexually fulfillment, and always put himself first. And women love every second of it. You would find romance novels about the devoted loving husband and father flying off the shelves. Yet the ones featuring dominant, often damaged, assholes sell like hotcakes. I'm sure women and their enablers have convenient politically correct "reasoning" for why this is but the fact of the matter is bad boys get women wet.

A woman will turn down a guy who will be devoted to her, cares about her, and treats her as an equal go and get her brains banged out by a guy who literally care less about her who tosses her out like used rag afterwards, and do it time and time again while complaining about guys being assholes or if she could just find a nice devoted guy all the time. It's as consistent as night following day. It has been this way since the beginning and will be this way for all times.

A Woman's Insatiable Need

Women have a hard time controlling their sexuality. Women are not known for being sturdy and consistent. Line up one hundred men tempt them with something they want and let's say fifty give in. Line up one hundred women and tempt them with something they want and ninety nine will give in. This applies to sexuality as well. While women's level of base line horniness or base line sexual drive isn't as high as a man's. Women will still give in whenever a man who is masculine takes them. Put another way women are easy. This isn't to put them down or say it in a pejorative way, it's simply a fact.

Women have an insatiable need for a strong masculine men between their legs. It doesn't matter if she's married, has a boyfriend, a hardcore feminist, or whatever. Biology trumps ideology and social constructs every time. They can't help nor do they want to. Add in their inherent disregard for consequences with social constructs that facilitate exonerating women from their consequences and any resistant to urges gives away completely. With no consequences for her actions a woman can indulge in their desires even more so than before. Which they are doing at a record amount. Even when women were stoned for adultery many women still couldn't resist men, now with adultery seen as the man's fault and women given one hundred and one reasons why she's not the blame and this dynamic is going to grow even more.

These truths might not be pleasant but they are truths. Pursue the truth, it may be bitter going down, but it is the only healthy foundation you can build on.

One Of The Most Important Keys For Having Sex With A Woman

It's unfortunate but most guys struggle with women (among other things in life). Regardless of their goals the majority of men struggle. From having successful marriages to banging all the hotties they want very few males have the ideal sex life, very few males get all that they want out of life. It's unfortunate but it's true. However there are a select group of men who do know how to get what they want in life and with women among other things. That men that occupy that highest rung of the sexual pyramid. The twenty percent of men who get eighty percent of women or whatever the statistic is. These men understand that the number one key to having sex with lots of beautiful women has to do with having an emotional impact.

While having a successful marriage takes a lot more, having sex with beautiful women does not. Learn how to impact a woman's emotions and you'll never be sleeping alone (except of course when you want to). Sounds nice doesn't it? Bringing home that hottie from the bar when you want, banging that girl in class who always wears the short shorts, or picking up that hot business woman from the conference. It all comes down to this thing and this thing is having an emotional impact. For one night stands and quick lays this is your number one goal, to have an emotional impact on a woman.

How To Make An Emotional Impact On A Woman

Making an emotional impact on a woman isn't hard. For starters you cannot care or be afraid of her reaction, let me repeat that. Her reaction should not deter you. You need to hold your frame completely and unashamedly. You will get tested but you should know how to pass those. Don't give in to her test. Regardless of how she reacts you must hold the frame. This is the foundation upon which having an emotional impact is made, a weak man will have trouble making an emotional impact because he will give in too quickly and therefore any attraction and intrigue created will quickly dissipate.

I've talked about teasing women before and related it to a balloon. Where women walk around with inflated balloons where most men come up to them and pump more air into the balloon (by lavishing praise and worship on them usually) which just bores women and turns them off. Compare that with a guy who goes up and busts her chops or tease he a little popping the balloon and getting her attention. The guy who "insults" a woman is going to have a much bigger emotional impact than the guy who gets on his knees and compliments her.

Can Be Positive Or Negative

This may surprise you but your emotional impact does not have to be positive, it can be negative and still have a strong effect. Of course you need to strive for some sort of balance as well as positive is usually preferred but even negativity is preferred over indifference. Indifference is the death of attraction there must tension and emotions involved. Negative emotions are better than no emotions by a long shot. As a matter of fact sometimes used in the right way using negative emotions can be even more beneficial than using positive emotions.

Let's look at the backhanded compliment and why it is so effective. It causes two kinds of emotional spikes both positive and negatives. This combination of the two makes it doubly effective. It causes positive emotion by being a compliment but also negative emotions by being backhanded. They will tell you all you need to know about effectively using the backhanded compliment.

The Number One Factor

When it comes to one night stands and quick lays having an emotional impact is the number one factor involved. Give women emotional impacts and keep them coming and you will not be going home alone. Having an emotional impact is also important in long term relationships as well it just isn't the number one factor. No matter who you are or what your intentions are it's important that you learn how to have an emotional impact on a woman and are not scared to do so. All you need to do is have an emotional impact and you can get laid a lot. Like all a woman has to do is look good to have sex with the guys she wants all a man has to do is have an emotional impact.

This is the number one key to having lots of one night stands with good looking women. Do this combined with keeping the other principles in this book in mind and presenting yourself properly and you'll never have trouble at a bar or out on the town again. Remember getting laid is simple not complicated. It doesn't require a lot and far too many males spend way too much time on this subject when it is easy to master. Remember women (or a woman) should never be your number one priority and never be the focus of your life. Regardless if your banging a different woman every night or with the love of your life. A woman/women is never the focus.

What Women Want & Only Men Can Fulfill

I've stated before that ideology does not override biology. It matters little if this ideology is religion, social movements, or a political party biology triumphs over them all. We all know plenty of born again sluts, girls who profess to be feminists yet get their rocks off with the most manly asshole they can find, occupy Wall-Streeters who would jump at a chance with their own Christian Greys and so on and so forth. Women will always submit to strength and power and always be attracted to it.

Just like a man could pretend like he thinks blonde girls measuring 36-24-36 walking around in skimpy bikinis is "disgraceful" or "misogynist" or whatever he's been programmed to say. Yet unless he has a mental disease he is going to be attracted to them. Attraction is not a choice. A woman can no more control her attraction to strength, power, and masculine energy than a man can to curves, long hair, and feminine energy. You can only ignore this reality at your own peril. There are certain things that women want and only men can fulfill and whatever man can fulfill this women will gravitate towards. Even if it's a man they profess to hate. Here are just some of women's needs that only men can fulfill.

The Need To Submit

All women have a need to submit to a man stronger than they are, preferably much stronger. When the males around her are not strong a woman will find something or someone else to submit too. This could be the drug dealer a few blocks over or it could be a popular ideology like feminism or it could be whatever the media tells her to. The reason being these ideologies give off the illusion of strength because a) most males are a bunch of panty-wastes who would never contradict the mainstream way of thinking and b) because of this they believe this ideology to be strong.

Of course is a strong man comes into her life that ideology will fly out the window but the ideology sort of acts as a placeholder until a woman can find a real man (if she ever does). If not she'll be angry and bitter her whole life because she will never be fulfilled. Because despite feminism saying that women find fulfillment through working a career, hating men, cheap wine, and cats that truth is women only find their fulfillment through supporting a man, submitting to a man, and raising a man's children.

Lost In You

Women want to be lost in the man they are with. They want to be so enraptured in his masculine energy that they can feel their feminine energy fully and completely. They want to get lost in you and your manliness. They want to look up to as their fearless leader who they would follow into hell because they trust in your strength. You must be her king and she your doting queen. At least that is her ultimate desire and the closer she can get to that the better she is going to feel. Women don't want control and they don't want to take the lead and they feel bitter and shitty when they do have to.

Women want to get lost in your dominance. A man is the only thing that can truly and fully meet this need. Everything else is either a cheap substitute or straight up poison designed to keep women unfulfilled, bitter, and angry. This was something that society used to know and respect before it became infected by the cancer that holds it now. Women will never be fulfilled by their career, by riding the cock carousal, or by anything else the media/feminist tells them will fulfill them. Only a man can fulfill them and make them feel complete.

Women Want Sex

Women want sex especially with masculine men. However women (for the most part) will not initiate it and many will walk around annoyed and unfulfilled instead of coming on to a man them self. This is because women are supposed to be pursued not the pursuer (again for the most part) and a woman who has to make the first move feels a) like she isn't very desirable as a woman if she has to do so and b) that if she has to make a move on a male he must be very weak or insecure to not make the move himself.

Of course if you're at the top of the sexual pyramid women will throw themselves at you but that's because you're the top alpha so to speak. What I'm saying is many women walk around horny and unfulfilled and are just waiting for a man with balls enough to be forward with her to take her and ravish her. She wants to be screwed and be screwed good. Cheap romance novels and toys will not fulfill her only a man's passion can do that. Most males are to scared to be forward with a woman (and also be honest), most males are too scared to fulfill a woman's needs. That's too bad for them, good thing you know better. Most women go crazy without dick.

Summary

This all comes down to one thing, women need men. Women need men for a variety of reasons too many to list in one chapter or even one book. Feminist is a weak veneer over a bunch of scared little girls who are angry because men aren't calling them on their bullshit, putting them in their place, and fulfill them like they want to be fulfilled. Like everything focus on being a man and all that entails then everything else will fall into its place.

How To Get Hypergamy To Work In Your Favor

It's no secret that the harsh reality of hypergamy has ruined more than a few males lives. Hypergamy is put shortly a woman's desire to have the highest quality man that she can. A common example is a woman cheating on her dedicated beta husband of twenty years whom she has two kids with for a random biker she met at the bar. Because the biker was more masculine and dominant and therefore of higher value than her loyal beta husband.

Hypergamy has created plenty of angry, hateful, males. Who upon discovering the reality of women became bitter and angry because they found that they had been lied too and their illusion was shattered. Usually by finding another man in their girl. This experience can certainly be harsh and a certain period of anger is natural. However there comes a time when a man has to dust himself off and soldier on becoming better and stronger.

Biology Isn't Fair

Unfortunately most males go on looking for some sort of fairness from the world. They've been burnt where is their recompense? This cannot be said enough but there is no recompense. There is no fairness in the world, there is simply reality. This isn't something to whine and cry about (which real men never do) but rather something to understand and then operate from this new understanding. Hypergamy and female nature simply are.

Once you understand it then you can use it to your advantage. But you have to let go of your fantasies first. There is no one loyal woman just waiting for you. Women want the top alpha guys and the beta settle for the scraps, that's reality. There is no room in the middle anymore like there was in the 50's. Just like the middle class will be gone in 25 years so will the sexual middle class so to speak. You'll either be a 1% or a loser, those are the choices.

Making Hypergamy Work In Your Favor

Something many males, especially the angry bitter ones (which MGTOW and the red pill have plenty of unfortunately) never understand that once you raise your rank on the sexual pyramid that all those things that worked against them before now work for them.

Now women (even "committed" married ones) will seek them out for sex and adventure. The tables have turned once you go from beta to alpha. Just like when you go from middle class to upper class.

You become a man instead of a whipping boy. Look self-development isn't a choice. Either learn to fight or don't cry when the wolves of reality tear you to shreds. I know what you're thinking "but this isn't fair" "But my parents/teachers/preachers/politicians/other liars & idiots told me otherwise". Look man, this is reality. And the thing about reality is you can either embrace it and live a successful life or ignore it and get shafted because of that ignorance. Ignorance is not bliss but knowledge is power.

Grow Everyday

So in order to get hypergamy to work for you, you have to go from beta to alpha, from loser to winner, from dud to stud. This is going to require you getting your shit together and working on yourself until you reach that rank. This is going to require you to master the basic skills of manhood. In particular it is going to require you to root out any weakness that you may have as well as embracing your dominance.

This type of growth is accomplished just like any other kind of growth.

Hypergamy can be made to work in your favor when you rise above the level of average and to that of the successful. You are going to have to grow and grow fast. It'll be hard but it will be worth it. As males we can either rise and soar like the eagle or we will be kicked to wayside and be trodden upon by society. There is no middle on the road option and when you think there is you are simply doing yourself a disservice by ignoring reality.

Summary

Seek knowledge and take action. That is how growth happens. If you haven't read books about the nature of women then do so and then test your new found knowledge out in the world. You'll be pleasantly surprised how well things work once you understand the game and have it working in your favor. The road is hard but the reward is more than worth it. Develop yourself and before you know it hypergamy will be working in your favor.

Is There Such Thing As A Lesbian?

Woman was made for man. This is the natural order and how biologically humans are supposed to function. While there is no doubt in my mind that woman's sexuality is much more fluid than men's still there is much that I question about women who claim to be lesbians. You see all women want men. Not boys or pussies but men. Real men.

This isn't an option. It's hardwired into a woman's system. And sure there are many things that can affect a woman's system. Society, programming, mental diseases, and so on and so forth. Yet at the end of the day woman want men.

So in answer to is there such thing as a lesbian my response would be for the most part not really. Let me explain.

The Truth

A woman may say she is a lesbian for a variety of reasons. The top ones being that she can't get a man, she's been hurt by many men, and she wants attention. However even with these outside events women still retain their normal brain functioning. They still have the same biological makeup that they had before they decided to make a change. They are still attracted to men, regardless if they will deny this or not.

It reminds me of women who say they hate jerks yet blow a different jerk every weekend. You can say whatever you want sweetheart but actions speak a hell of a lot louder than words. It is because they biologically wired to men who are often considered jerks. TV, their friends, and society may tell them they want wimpy sensitive nice guys who are pro-Feminist and woman may believe that they do however that doesn't follow that woman want sensitive nice guys even if they do sleep with a couple of them (generally in a relationship until they cheat on them with a bad boy).

I should note that bull dykes are excluded from what I'm talking about her. I am referring to women that still hold any semblance of their feminine nature. Tatted up, short haired bull dykes obviously do not fall into this category. I mean lesbian women who still have their femininity intact, even if it's barely intact.

Converting

I've discovered that it is incredibly easy to uh "convert" the vast majority of lesbians that I meet. A woman saying she is a lesbian seems to matter just as much as her having a boyfriend (aka not that much). If you are a man woman have an undeniable attraction to you. Old women, young women, Feminist women, conservative women, Muslim women, bar sluts, strippers, church wives, soccer moms, high school girls, college girls, the next door neighbor. All of them. All women love and want a real man. Even if they deny it or are not consciously aware of it. Trust me showing them your masculinity opens up something deep and primal in them. Like pouring lighter fluid on a dying flame.

Here's the dynamic with most lesbians. So you have the bull dyke and then the relatively feminine one (the ones I'm talking about in this chapter). The relatively feminine one is with the bull dyke because of her faux masculinity. Sort of like how a man would rather look at porn than nothing yet sex with a real woman is so much better. Porn is faux sex. Meaning a cheap replacement which is what bull dykes are for real men. A cheap replacement.

When a woman is exposed to real masculinity suddenly

something is awakened in her. Bull dykes are generally more faux masculine than your average male in Western society (how sad is that?) so a woman can be around her male friends and be lesbian and not feel anything. Yet put this same woman around a guy like me and everything changes.

Undeniable Attraction

Biology trumps disease of both the mind and society of which lesbianism is one. And I thank God for that. Biology and the natural order trumps all. It always wins in the end. So when you base your actions and belief off of it you will always come out in the right. While pissing off all those who base their beliefs in the delusions of the day.

Women cannot help but respond to masculinity.
Your masculine dominance. Next time you hear "she's a lesbian" smirk and shrug it off like you would anything else. Treat it like a shit test and you'll be golden. Remember there is no such thing as a true lesbian (except bull dykes).

Why It Doesn't Matter If A Girl Has A Boyfriend

Ever been at a bar and heard one of your buddies say about the women in the place "They're all with guys" or something to that extent. The exact phrasing isn't what matters (it never is) the point is that men often disqualify themselves for a variety of reasons, the majority of which do not have any bearing on reality. Here I want to address one of the most popular ones. Namely if a girl is with a guy at a bar/club/wherever then they are off limits are either don't want to be talked to or something to that extent. When in reality nothing could be further from the truth.

Why It Doesn't Matter

Let's start with the basics. Many guys think that when a woman is out with a guy that it is most likely their boyfriend (as if that would matter to the woman anyways) and therefore they shouldn't go talk to them. This is generally false. Women sometimes go out with their boyfriends but what you are most likely seeing at a bar is a woman out with her beta orbiters looking for a real man to satisfy her. While the beta orbiter's keep the free drinks and compliments coming. These men are generally just emotional tampons that the woman uses for validation, while real men are what get her rocks off.

In addition to if a woman finds a man who she is more attracted to than the man she is with, the man she is with ceases to matter. This is true when the other man is her boyfriend or husband how much more true is it when it's just some dude who hopes lavishing her with drinks and attention will get him in her pants? I remember in college many girls who boyfriends went to another school who were dying for me to have sex with them because they wanted me one hundred times more than their boyfriends. Many women wouldn't even bring up if they had a boyfriend/husband and when one of their friends did they were given the eyes of death and chastisement from the woman who I was talking with. So either way it doesn't matter. If you want a woman that is what matters. Now I would advise staying away from married and taken women obviously but what I'm saying is if you see a girl and you want her go for it. If it turns out she's married or taken then find another but don't just assume.

An Excuse

This of course could have another meaning depending on the guy who says it. This could also mean "I'm too scared to approach women so I'm going to rationalize it by saying that they're all with guys". An excuse is an excuse and bitching out is bitching out, you can dress it up any way you choose it's still the same. The worst excuses are those who seem to have some rationality to them (doesn't matter their still excuses). Excuses are cancerous to your manhood. There are few things that will destroy it more.

Excuses are what the weak use to justify sucking. Even if an excuse sounds right in your head realize it's still an excuse and is still poison. Imagine if they put rat poison in a colorful box with a cartoon rat on the front and the USDA said it was part of a balanced meal. It looks right and the USDA would never lie right? After all they are part of the government which always has our best interest at heart. Poison is poison no matter how palatable or pretty it looks or sounds.

Limiting Thoughts

Limiting thoughts are a pernicious sickness. Remember your mindset is the most important facet of your life. Your mind being poisoned is like a well being poisoned during a siege. With the water gone all is lost. With your mind poisoned all is lost. Your mind is the beginning and the end of where you will end up in life. You were given this gift and now it is your duty and responsibility to make the very most out of it.

You must declare war on any weak and limiting thoughts. Such as I can't approach a woman because there is a man out with her. You like a woman you approach her that's that. No excuses, no buts, nothing. Put in caveman terms you want, you do. Treat you limiting thoughts like barbarians treated those they conquered. No mercy, no quarter.

Now what are you waiting for? She's waiting…

2 Things That Most Guys Don't Understand That Keeps Them From Having The Sex Life They Want

Many males have this fantasy of a woman seducing themselves for them. Meaning that a woman is just so enraptured and turned on by him that she jumps on him and rips off his pants like in the movies. Thanks to the weakness of modern males combined with negative influences such as movies, songs, and especially pornography many males have bought into this fantasy thinking it's the real thing. They think if they look good, dress nice, and smile women will be grabbing them and taking them behind corners or into bedrooms doing all the work themselves.

This allows the male to be passive and weak yet still sleep with attractive women. This reminds me of the fantasy of a fat woman being seduced by a rich handsome studly guy or a old career cat lady who guys throw themselves at. A fantasy that has no bearing on reality and is a matter of fact the opposite of reality. Playing coy and being a weak wimp is a guaranteed way to always end up with your hand at the end of the night just like being fat or a career women is a turn off for men. Here are two principles to understand to get rid of this faulty programming society shoves down our throats and that will get you laid a whole lot more.

Principle #1 – You Must Show Interest First

A woman even if deep down she wants you to bend her over and give it to her like never before isn't going to be too overt about this. The most you'll get is a smile or maybe some eye contact and even then even is she's really attracted to you sometimes you won't even get that. Women are very convert and don't want to appear easy or like a slut. Some don't mind but even those the most they'll do is put their hands on you and laugh a lot. Even the most bold of women that's about all they are going to do. Women also have huge egos and don't want to be embarrassed.

If a guy approached a woman and she doesn't reciprocate his interest it's no big deal. Guys are supposed to start the interaction and he still has his pride because he had the balls to go for it and everyone deep down knows this. However if a woman showed interest to a guy and was rejected it would be incredibly embarrassing for her. This has to do with biological traits that would require a book in and of themselves to explain. The man must show interest first to make it safe for the woman to return the interest. The man makes the first move and leads in every part of the interaction. From hello to sex. Even when the man shows interest the woman will still play coy she isn't going to suddenly reciprocate at the same level.

Principle #2 – A Woman Will Never Seduce Herself For You

A woman will never seduce herself for you. Meaning she isn't going to grab you rip off your pants and drop to her knees and start bobbing back and forth. Ever. Even if she wants nothing more in the world to bang you she is going to wait for you to make that possible. Seduction for men is an active thing. Women aren't active in the seduction. Even if you are the studliest of studs and a woman gets wet and can't even control herself or think in your presence you still need to be the one who makes the moves and leads the interaction to sex, she's not going to do it herself.

You are the active force in the seduction the woman is the passive. She might say hi, get one of her friends to tell you she thinks you're cute, smile and wave, stand near you, or touch your arm when she laughs but that's about it. Most guys are waiting for her to push them down on a bed and mount them before thinking "Hey this girl wants me" and that's why they'll never get laid. You have to be the one taking action and being aggressive. You're the man. A woman isn't going to seduce herself for you.

Summary

Where this line of thought comes from I'm not sure whether it movies where the nerdy guy is seduced by the babe because he's so cute or pornography where essentially the same thing happens. Get that shit out of your mind. Those fantasies only exist in movies, not in real life. I see so many guys sitting around waiting for women to make the first move. It isn't going to happen pal, you're the man you take action. You make the first move and all the subsequent moves as well. Understanding this is going to more than triple the amount of women that you sleep with. So show interest first and take the lead, because a woman will never seduce herself for you and do all the work for a myriad of reasons. Be a man and everything falls into place.

From Hello To Sex In 3 Easy Steps

Getting laid isn't that hard despite most males thinking the opposite. Attracting women and having sex with them is a natural biological act. It results from the attraction created stemming from the polarization between the masculine and the feminine. Most males approach getting laid as if it's some grand play that takes years of study and hard work then requires tons of energy to perform. While the marketers in the industry of "getting girls" would love to have you believe that. The truth of the matter is having sex with the women you want has more in common with sleeping, walking, and using the restroom than it does great works of art or industry.

It's a simple basic biological function. Something so basic and honestly minuscule in the grand scheme of life that it should never take priority. Now many of you are probably thinking "Alright Sledge if it's so easy then why the hell do the vast majority of men struggle with this?". Now we're on to something. Look at it the same way as being in decent shape, meaning not obese. Meaning you can do normal functions. It's not that hard to not be obese yet if you looked at the average Westerner you'd think it was a huge struggle, when the fact of the matter is it isn't.

Step One – Be A Man

The reasons that the average Western is obese is because they are divorced from a natural lifestyle and eating habits, which aren't that hard to follow and when they are followed result in a healthy weight. Likewise most males have trouble having sex with the women they want because they have no masculinity within them. Their masculine has been attacked and sheered away to the point that there is nothing less (especially if they were "raised" by a single mother). These males have no innate masculinity and therefore nothing to cause polarization or attraction with women. And even when women are interested in them, they don't have the balls to escalate and go for it.

Without this inner masculinity the outer things aren't going to matter. There will be no polarization. To succeed with women you need to have a masculine frame that you operate from. You must be man to woman as God and nature intended. You must have a masculine core that radiates out from you. It's something women can sense. From your eyes, to the way you carry yourself, to everything else. Masculinity is noticed and women cannot help but be helplessly attracted to it. After all there is no competition for masculine men.

Step Two – Get Her Emotionally Engaged

Women are emotional creatures that are entirely controlled by their emotions. This is a fact. To get a woman to sleep with you you need to engage her emotions. You are better off pissing her off then boring her. Even negative emotions are one hundred times better than no emotions at all.

You do this by always having the stronger frame and teasing women. Call them out on their bullshit, mess with them, treat them like you're the man and they're the silly little girl. Because in reality that's exactly what it is. Have fun with her and be a source of fun.

This doesn't mean be a clown. Clowns are weak and don't operate from a masculine core. It means have fun and don't take her seriously (why would you take a woman seriously?). Get her emotionally engaged with you by spiking her emotions. Make fun of her in a playful way. You're the boss she's the silly little girl. I know I'm repeating myself but I want to make sure you understand the dynamic. You're the man she's the woman. This is the best way to have an emotional impact which is key to sleeping with the women you want.

Step Three – Escalate Physically

If you don't touch a woman you aren't going to have sex with her, it's as simple as that. You could have her raring to go but if you don't escalate physically it's just going to end up in blue balls for you and anger mixed with frustration for her. Something no one wants. You have to touch her. Women want and love to be touched by a masculine man (this is a vast understatement like men like getting blow jobs from blondes with double D's and nice asses). Touch is key here. Even after her emotions are engaged and you're operating from a masculine core, nothing's going to happen until you take the lead and begin physically escalating on her.

This is also something that should come naturally but our society has neutered it out of most males. Think about what's more natural than a guy touching a woman he's attracted to? Not much. Most of this has to do with undoing the poison society injects into males and getting in touch with our masculine core. Being natural. Always keep this in mind if you're as masculine guy who has spiked a woman's emotions then she is waiting for you to touch her. Hell if you're just a masculine guy she's probably waiting for you to touch her. Never underestimate the power of touch.

From Hello To Sex

So there you have it from hello to sex in three easy steps, and it wasn't even cheesy. Follow these three steps and you'll never have to worry about not sleeping with the women you want again. Having the sex life you want is an important part of a man's life. It's an incredibly strong (and fun) biological desire and as long as it doesn't crowd out what really matters then you're good. Like I've said before once you truly become a man, fully and completely. Then everything else falls into place.

2 Universal Needs Of Women

Though every human is a technically a unique creature we all share a common biology. Which is why learning things like evolutionary psychology is so important. Because there is a basis that we all work from. All humans also have the capacity to forge their own lives. Humans are unique in that unlike animals they can work against their biology and become something above the level of an animal. Of course this requires discipline and self-management and the truth is the majority of people will never be anything more than biologically animals…sheep.

With this being said all women share a common biology and that means that even with all their differences they have universal needs. Needs that can only be filled by a man and not by anything else. The same can be said of men but this chapter is going to focus on the universal needs of women. All women share these needs. Sure they may deny them hell they might not even be aware of them. But nevertheless they are there. It's biology and biology holds stronger sway than ideology, never forget that. Do women differ of course yet they still all operate from the same base.

Even the jaded "I don't need no man"/"Fish bicycle!" type woman will submit to a dominant man she's been craving deep down despite all rhetoric against it. Hell most angry bitchy women are just mad no man desires them enough to dominate them, much less dominate and then care for them. At the end of the day men want women and women want men. The sexes were made to complement one another but have been turned against one another because when the populace is divided they are easier to conquer. Now let's get to those desires.

To Be Desired

All women want to be desired. They want to be wanted. They want men to want them. All women want this. It doesn't matter their race, age, or anything else, they all want to be desired by men. Of course ultimately they want to be desired by a strong masculine men yet just about any desire is better than no desire. Hence the "beta orbiters" she keeps around to stave off feeling completely unwanted while looking for a real man to truly fulfill this desire as only a strong man can.

Women want to have strong masculine men have animalistic passion and desire for them. They want men, in particular alpha men to want to possess them. They want to see men have animalistic passion for them. That's why the whole "be aloof and never show a woman you want her ever/always be indirect and hide your sexual desire" is the dumbest thing I can think of. It's a guaranteed way to either never get laid or make it one hundred times harder than it needs to be. Women want to be wanted by real men.

They want to be possessed, taken, and ravished by men who have the capacity to do so.

Dangerous masculine men. They want to feel a man's passion. To feel his desire and want and know that she is the cause of it. To know that she can cause such strong emotions in a strong dominant man. Women want to be wanted by men. They want to be wanted period, but strong men are obviously the preferred one. Like a man would rather have sex with a super model than some plain chick at school. Yet at the end of the day would rather have sex with the plain chick than his hand. Women work in similar ways other than they don't give sex to the beta orbiters the way a man would give sex to the plain woman.

They Want To Experience Passion

Women are not self-starters. They are not an active force they are a reactive force. It is the masculine that is the active force. Women feel what others make them feel, especially men. They cannot facilitate these feelings on their own. A vibrator can never replace a man (to the irk of many Feminists and career women). Sex and desire is very emotional for women. While with a man sex often comes down to friction and physics with women it comes down to psychology and is mostly a mental game.

A woman cannot inspire passion in herself, she needs a man to do so. Most women are starved for passion and when I sat starved I mean haven't eaten in forty days literally an hour from death starved. Their lives are boring and droll. They cannot create their own fun and adventure like a man but must rather go along with the fun and adventure of others. Of course this is easier said than done. A woman wants to be swept up by a man's desire and passion and become a part of his world.

Dominance is the first requirement and then care. If a wimpy male cares for a woman it means nothing like if a land whale wants to sleep with you. So fucking what? However dominance is more important than care. If a woman has to choose between a man who can only dominate her and a man who can only care about her, she's going to pick the only dominate every time. Care only matters when held up by the foundation of dominance/masculinity. Sort of like if you had to choose between a fat girl who was submissive and a blond doll who was bitchy you would pick the blonde doll. However the ultimate desire if for both, however dominance is the stronger of the two.

Summary

Learning about human biology and psychology is important for living a successful happy life. When you go against biology you get burned. Look at how most in the West live unfulfilled, pain filled lives. Because they have gone against the natural order and are crushed by it. Reality isn't going to change for you, you can only adapt yourself to it. Show open and full desire for a woman, don't be coy. Don't play those little boy games "Where'd you get your shoes?" "Who lies more men or women" or any stupid stuff like that. Be a man and be open and unapologetic.

Leave the little boy games to males who don't want to get laid or have fulfilling relations with women. Be a man. Dominate her and show desire for her. Fulfill the two needs listed above and she will love you for it. A man who can fulfill a woman's needs is addicting to her, especially in this age of man-boys, pussies, and wimps. You were created man for a reason, to be fully and completely a man. In every area when you do this women, children, society everything will be drawn to you. And most important of all you will have reconnected with the deepest part of yourself your manhood and

your life will never be the same
after.

You're Already More Than Enough For Any Woman

There are many things in life that you are going to have to earn. Things like money, honor, respect from other men, strength, victory in combat, and many others. However one thing that you don't have to earn and are in fact already enough for is the most beautiful women in the world (and all the others as well) you see simply by the fact that you are a man you are already more than enough for any woman. And a man who knows this arouses desire in every woman because he knows his true place. You are already more than enough for any woman.

Deep down all women know this and honestly deep down I think all men know this too. You don't have to earn women through anything they are all already available to you. While you may have to work for years to be a championship fighter or own that house you've always wanted or have complete freedom in life, the most beautiful women are already available to you. You are already more than enough for them. A man who realizes this will have no problems attracting women even if he's out of shape, broke, and whatever else many males consider to make them not worthy of women (what a joke).

Indoctrination

Males are taught since birth that they are inferior to females. There are a couple of reasons for this. First and foremost weak males are easy to control and don't cause trouble. So society seeks to make a world of neutered slaves to control as they will. Also by telling men women are worth more it blinds men to the fact that they are already more than enough for any woman. Otherwise men wouldn't seek to get women through money, the gym, or other means they would simply go straight for the woman they wanted (and get them).

If men found out that just by being a man that they're already entitled to the most beautiful women (and therefore all below that as well) it's throw a big ol monkey wrench in the machine used to push society "forward". Men would stop mindlessly working jobs they hate, they'd stop putting up with so much bullshit, they'd stop being mindless consumers. Not exactly good for business or good for those in power. So the myth that men require something outside of themselves to get women is pushed harder and harder.

You're Already More Than Enough

Don't get me wrong just because you're more than enough for any woman doesn't mean to sit on your ass. There are things far far more important than women in this life. Most males never realize this unfortunately. Most because they never get the women they want and so always chase something that will never fulfill them in the first place. Not that women don't play a part in a man's life because they certainly do. But anyways back to the topic at hand. You are entitled to the best women simply by being a man. You're already more than enough.

This cannot be said enough. You don't need money, big muscles, height, a suit, or whatever all you need is you and your masculinity. A man who understands he is entitled to the best women is going to turn women on like crazy, it's as simple as that. Because he realizes his inherent worth as a man. The man is the prize. Repeat this to yourself one hundred times a day if you have to but "You're already more than enough for any woman". Any, never forget this. Simply by just being a man you are already more than enough for any woman.

False Strategies

I'm aware that I'm repeating myself. But this is something that it's hard for many males to grasp. It goes counter to what they've been told their entire lives even though it is the truth. This is why you see women who think that if they act like they're entitled to men that men will find them attractive when in fact they find them repulsive. A woman is using the wrong sexual strategy. Just like when men think if they're in good shape, tanned, and have nice hair that they'll attract women.

That's not how it works. This is what happens when you raise the sexes to think that they are the same. Mass confusion. A woman tries that because that's what makes a man attractive to her likewise men try that because that's what makes women attractive to them. You have each sex using the other's strategy then wondering why it's not working. Men are already more than enough for any woman, it doesn't work the other way around. Might not be fair (though biologically everything ends up being "fair") but it's the truth.

Summary

Now there are things you will have to earn in this life and must work toward. Freedom being the number one thing. However women are not one of these things. You are already more than enough for any woman that has ever lived and will ever live simply because you are a man. Never forget this. You are already more than enough. Don't get caught up in thinking you have to earn women, you don't. Again say it with me you're already more than enough. Alright I think you got it, now go live it.

How To Get More Ass Than A Toilet Seat

Seduction can seemingly be a complicated process. But the fact of the matter is it's actually pretty simple and easy. First off to put it lightly there are more than one way to skin a cat. Meaning that there are many different methods, principles, and such that work. Sure they may vary in their effectiveness overall and some will be better for different personality types than others but at the end of the day a good portion of them work. It isn't rocket science it's putting your dick in a girl. The most basic of biological needs.

With that being said there are some principles that apply across all methods and that you should be aware of. This isn't a chapter about them but just something you should be aware of. I've written about a couple of different methods myself such as spiking a woman's emotions, being a dominant masculine man, and being a bad boy. And truth be told all work and all work well and they work even better when you know how to combine them all for maximal effectiveness (but that's not something to worry about right now). In this chapter I'm going to talk about another way in which you can start getting more ass than a toilet seat.

The Battle Of Frames

First off realize that everything have to do with attraction is based in biology. And that our biology is based in living in tribal times when the threat of getting eaten or killed by another tribe was the number one thing occupying our minds. Anything that would add to this survival is going to cause attraction. When you look at it like that is simplifies all of this greatly. Women being the weaker of the two species are even more aware of this than men. Not consciously obviously but subconsciously. Hence shit tests and the like. One requirement of seduction is that the man have the stronger frame than the woman.

Frame is incredibly important in seduction (and in life). Women naturally have weak frames and value men with strong ones to make up for their weakness. A strong frame is more important than looks, money, or whatever else you are attaching your self-worth to. She wants to submit to you and she can't if you don't have a more dominant frame than her. Look at it this way in order for her to become attracted to you you have to be stronger than her and this all starts with having the stronger frame. It's the foundation upon which everything else is built.

You Are Dominant

You need to have the "I am dominant" frame. Not domineering but dominant. Domineering comes from being a try hard and weakness while dominance comes from masculinity and strength. You have to be strong, calm, and collected in the face of adversity. This includes when she tests you to see if you are an attractive man who she'll want to have sex with. If you cower before a girl with a nice ass who tells you to go away what use are you going to be when a sabretooth tiger attacks the camp? Remember attraction is a primal/biological function.

As long as you have a stronger frame than the woman you are going to be good. You don't have to be perfect, just enough. And you already are enough for any girl out there. I don't say that as some "woo woo" bullshit but as a fact of reality. You're a man, you're already enough. Your frame must dominate hers from attraction (and sex) to occur. Meaning you can't give in to pressure from her, her friends, or anything around you.

You should completely ignore any social pressure, the more pressure you can withstand without flinching the stronger you prove yourself to be and therefore the more attracted she is going to be to you.

Never Fazed

If you're not man enough to dominate a pretty girls frame with your own then you have such a weak frame she'll never be attracted. This includes her ignoring you at first, telling you to go away, telling you you're too X, and so on and so forth. So what, some chick is telling you things you're a man why the hell would you listen? Have balls and just keep doing what you're doing. When you give in you prove you're a pussy and the woman will lose all attraction to you. Likewise the more resistance she throws your way that doesn't faze you and you overcome the hotter she's going to get for you.

Just stay in there, don't be fazed, and keep doing what you do. Eventually she'll realize you are actually a man with balls who has a strong frame (like finding a diamond in a coal mine for her) and her frame will give in to yours and she'll want you to screw her brains out all night long. A win win for everyone around. But you never get here if you give in to her pressure, you never get here is you're weak. Think about it from a biological standpoint. If your too weak to stand your ground against a girl who is no threat to you what use are you against real threats like invaders and giant predators?

Summary

Be a man with balls and women will fall at your feet. You have to stay in there, stop turning away at the slightest sign of resistance or pressure against you. Be like a mountain when the winds blow against it. No matter how hard the winds blow it's not going to do shit the mountain. Don't get fazed by some girl no matter how hot she is. If you're too weak to stand against a girl you're going to get killed in the real world. Look your ancestors wouldn't take crap from invading hordes or giant predators and you're going to take crap from a girl? Of course not, stand your ground, have the stronger frame, and you'll be getting more ass than a toilet seat.

How To Be A Natural With Women

What does it mean to be a natural with women? How is it different from non-natural? Is there a difference or is it just semantics? While if you really want to most things can come to semantics however I do agree that there are certain things that naturals do that set them apart from the person who strives to be better with women through games and routines.

Eventually if you do something enough you become a

natural at it. You can walk right, if an alien came down from space and observed you they would probably think that you are a natural walker yet that's not the case. Through much trial and error were you able to walk. So much of being a natural is kids who took a risk and got some sort of reward stimulus from it. Maybe a parent praised them or they got some other form a reward then took that mindset into adulthood. Regardless here is a foundation for you to be a natural with women.

Sense Of Entitlement

Men who are naturals with women automatically know that

they are good enough for any woman. Doesn't matter if she's smoking hot, famous, or anything else. They are already more than enough for any woman that they cross paths with. They don't think any woman on this earth is better than them and honestly regard the idea as ridiculous. They have a high sense of self-worth and don't see any other way of living their life.

They'll go up to the smoking hot blonde that just blew out three guys and talk to her thinking nothing of it. They aren't caught in negative thoughts they have a positive thought patterns and a great attitude. The see the world as their personal playground to do with as they see fit. They are comfortable in any situation. They are at ease and relaxed. Beautiful women do not faze them because they know that they are already more than enough for any woman. They have nothing to prove to women.

Has Balls

Men who are naturals with women have balls which probably led to early positive reference experiences that they then continued throughout high school and on past there. They had some early success with women and then worked with that. A guy who is a natural with women does not mind taking risks. As a matter of fact he often seeks them out. Teasing gorgeous women he passes, having fun, he enjoys himself. He takes on the leadership role wherever he is and takes things where he wants them to go.

The natural always makes the first move as he understands how the sexes are supposed to operate. He never bought into the Feminist/societal social conditioning as his early reference experiences proved otherwise. He relates to women as a man. He takes the lead and leads the interaction where he wants it to go. He has his path and goes for it and anyone else who wants a good time is welcome to join him.

Masculine Core

The men who are naturals with women operate from masculine cores. They don't have to use routines or games to make up for anything as they have all that they need at their core. The thought of using underhand means and lines to pick up women would strike them as ridiculous and unnecessary. He doesn't need memorized words or phrases or whatever as he operates from a masculine core. He operates naturally and is not stifled by trying to act a certain way, he simply is a certain way that attracts women.

When a woman shit tests him it doesn't even register, he assumes that all women love and want him. He assumes attraction with every woman. Doesn't matter who or what she is, he assumes that she wants him. Doesn't mean he'd make a move on all of them obviously but he knows that they all want him at one level or another. He naturally is physical with women as I mean come on why wouldn't you touch women? And as physicality is the number one arousal factor with women this gets him a lot of good results.

Be A Natural With Women

You can be a natural with women. Everyone can. All behavior is learned. We enter this word with certain biological traits but not mental ones. Being a natural with women isn't some esoteric thing that you have to have the right genetics for. You can do whatever you set your mind too. Don't allow limiting thoughts to have a place in your life. Being a natural with women is about adopting certain behaviors men who learn game after internalizing it become natural with women.

Everything is a learned behavior don't forget that. From the way you walk, to the way you talk, to how you relate to the world around you. It can all be changed with enough work and desire for change. Remember your mind is the master. With it you can do anything other than change the laws of time and space. Focus it on your own life and you can make the changes you desire. Being a natural with women is no exception.

3 Lies That Men Believe About Women Debunked

In today's world we have generations of men that are brought up on lies about woman. In regards to how to relate to them, the importance that they should have in their life, what they want, and much more. Much of what popular mainstream culture spews about woman is lies designed to mislead men. Either in servitude or complete avoidance. Men nowadays either seem to think women are special holy oppressed creatures or that women are evil and should be avoided at all costs. Both unhealthy extremes but both having similar causes. Men being lied to about women.

The truth is the only foundation upon which a man can base his life. Regardless of the truth is painful or harsh. It doesn't matter, what matters is that you are building your foundation on truth. Any other foundation will fall out from underneath you at one point or another. When you build your house upon the sand of lies it will come tumbling apart when things get rough. But when you build your house on the hard rock of truth not even the strongest of storms will move it. The truth is what matters and it is the truth that men should pursue after.

Lie #1 – Women Don't Like Sex

This lie is usually pushed by jaded men and the mainstream thoughts on women (which are pretty much always wrong). You have angry bitter men who say all women want is money and that they'll just use sex to get it out of you. While yes when you are a beta and money is all you offer, yes women will use sex to get money off of you. But when you are a man and refuse to be a walking wallet, she's going to want you for other reasons.

Get it out of your head that woman only want money (or attention, or whatever). Don't get me wrong if a woman is not attracted to you she'll use you for these things but when you are an attractive man with game this changes. Women like sex just with certain men. While men want a woman as long as she is decent woman want men who are above them or have the appearance of being above them. They want men at the top of the sexual pyramid. So for all those men who think women don't sex, the truth is she probably does like sex just not with you. Work on yourself and change that to become a masculine man which all women love.

Lie #2 – Women Hate Submitting To Men

You've probably heard a guy joke about how his wife wears the pants and how she balks at any attempts of her submitting to him. Let me make something clear. This same woman who balks at the idea of submitting to her husband would submit wholeheartedly and become the servant of other attractive men. Women want to submit to men, granted they want them to be men worth submitting to (aka masculine men). Men who take charge and are naturally dominant. Not whipped little boys they can control and walk all over.

That same life who laughs in the face of her husband (or any submissive male) for that matter will get on her knees and pleasure a man who puts her in her place and do so joyfully. She's never not in the mood, just not in the mood for her husband or beta guys. Now this doesn't mean that a woman won't put up a fight or throw shit tests at a guy who doesn't take her crap. She will and when she sees that the guy is congruent (meaning actually a man who holds his ground and doesn't give into her) she will submit to him and love doing so.

Remember be a man and the woman will fall at your feet. Women were created to submit to men.

Lie #3 – Women Are Only Interested In Money

I addressed this one a bit in lie #1 but wanted to return to it here. This is something the vast majority of men, including so called "red pill" men have ingrained in them. That women just want men for their money. But's that not true. Like I said women just want boys who are easy marks for their money while they get their brains screwed out by guys who are actually men. When you use money as a way to attract women what you are doing is attracting women who are just going to use you for it. Granted if you do it well you can avoid this and use them but the majority of men end up victims of opportunistic women.

While the phrase men are only interested in sex is pretty much true (at least in regards to women) it is not true that women are only interested in money when it comes to men. Again, this is true only for boys and easy marks, not men. Look at it this way a woman will use her life savings to support a drunken delinquent who sleeps on the coach and bangs other women all day and then turn around and cheat on a rich guy with the delinquent and then take half the rich guys money when they divorce. Women are only interested in your money if that's all you got.

Summary

There could be a book written about all the lies the men are told about women with multiple volumes. This chapter simply addresses some of the top ones. Further your research into the ways that men and women work so that you do not end up a victim of lies. Remember the truth is the only foundation that is stable enough for you to base your life on. Anything else will give out on you at one time or another. You must base your life on the truth.

Women are interested in sex, they do want to submit to men, and they are not just interested in money. The key to all these are you must be an attractive man for these to hold true for you. If you are a rich wimp then yes all a woman is going to be interested in is your money. Specifically that she can take half when she leaves you for a man that gets her wet. It could be a broke bad boy or even a criminal so long as the man she goes with has his masculinity intact and functioning.

Can You Seduce A Woman With Eye Contact Alone?

Never ever underestimate the undercurrents of an interaction. What I mean by that is everything that is going on in an interaction other than the words said (which honestly barely matter at all). You do not seduce a woman through your words. Let me repeat that you do not seduce a woman through your words. You seduce her through your intentions and desires. Through your "vibe" which is created by your thoughts. That is how you seduce a woman. Touch and eye contact will "say" more to a woman than one thousand sonnets ever would or could. Words do not matter in seduction.

So can you seduce a woman with eye contact alone? Of course it's possible as just about everything is possible but that is not exactly what this chapter is going to be about. Eye contact says more than any other form of communication when you look a woman directly in the eyes unapologetically and without fear you are communicating to her on the deepest level possible. Not to sound flowery but you are communicating to her on a soul to soul level, a primal level. And the primal level is where sex is.

Eye Contact And Seduction

Eye contact is one of the best ways to communicate your desire to a woman and arouse her own desire for you. Women want to be wanted. When you want them and are unafraid to show it they want you back. Your eyes communicate what is within. And when you are a man who is unafraid of his desire you are going to communicate that to a woman. This isn't to brag simply to illustrate something but I have locked eyes with women and known that they wanted me that instant. I have found that the more forward and bold I am the better off I am.

Whenever I have tried to hide that desire it ended up with both me and the woman being unsatisfied. When you make eye contact with a woman do so without apology. Do not be the first to look away. The eye contact should be prolonged, direct, and intense. Looking back this and touch are the most effective methods of seducing women that I have found. Simply making strong eye contact, smiling seductively, and touching a woman with desire is enough to seal the deal.

Directed Thought

Now there may be some of you who are saying I make eye contact with women all the time and nothing is there. That would then be a problem with your desire. You must have sexual tension with women. This is conveyed through eye contact but only eye contact with directed thought behind it. This means you want to project your thoughts and sexual desire for a woman through your eyes into hers. Your thoughts are going to shine through when you make intense eye contact with a woman. Not a word by word replay obviously but the feeling, which is what matters anyways. Project that feeling, that primal desire you have for her into her eyes.

You want to project your masculine and sexual wants and desires to her. Hold nothing back. Communicate it all to her through your eyes. This is no time for inhibitions. Never underestimate what the eyes tell and what they convey. They are called windows into the soul for a reason. You can tell a lot by someone's eyes. I have looked men in the eyes and knew they were untrustworthy likewise I have looked men in the eyes and know they were with me to the death. With women I have looked into their eyes and seen unbridled lust waiting to be unleashed as well as a variety of other emotions.

Summary

Never underestimate the eyes. The words you say mean nothing compared to what you convey through your eye contact. The eyes can communicate more than words could ever hope to. Your intentions are going to shine through in your eyes and making intense prolonged eye contact. You should be making eye contact with everyone anyways but especially beautiful women you want to sleep with. Never be the first to look away.

You can go from looking intensely at a woman, to touching

her, to kissing her, to taking her home and screwing her without a word being said. Of course communication was still happening, more communication was happening in that situation than generally happens in hour long conversations. Eye contact and desire, never underestimate either one. They both have the potential to revolutionize your game. No one needs words or phrases to say when they have primal deep seduction.

Always Be Willing To Walk Away

It's pathetic the lengths that the average male will go to to win the affections of (aka sex with) women. What's even more pathetic is that their strategy all but guarantees that they will never be successful in their endeavors. Placating and appeasing women shows them without a shadow of a doubt that you are a weak man (you're letting her a little ole woman knock you off your game and boss you around). I mean after all from an evolutionary standpoint how strong can you be if you can't even stand up to a woman? Remember all of attraction stems from biological factors.

Which is why they test men. However most women go their whole lives without anyone ever calling them out on their bullshit (a great way to turn them on incidentally) and you end up with women who go from man to man or relationship to relationship getting angrier and more bitter because no one stands up to them and puts them in their place. They treat "men" like shit and then the "men" either stay with them or just take it not saying anything. I've seen men cheated on, talked down to, and ridiculed by girls they've been dating for a couple months and stick with it.

Raise You Attraction

For any kind of relationship to work between a man and woman attracted to each other the man has to be willing to walk away. It doesn't matter if it's a one night stand, dating, or a marriage. The man must always be willing to walk away. When a man is always willing to walk away the woman knows that is strong and therefore she'll want to screw him/stay with him. It'll make her attracted to you and know that you are a high value man. As you have standards for yourself and aren't weak. She knows that she can trust you to be a man which allows her to be a woman and also relate to you man to woman (that means sexually).

Imagine that every girl you met from afar looked like she had a wasp thin waist, a nice round booty, long pretty hair, and large breasts then as she got close to you and started talking to you her waist expanded, her breasts deflated, and her booty drooped. You'd lose attraction to her. Well that's how it is with women. They see a guy think he might be attractive but then he acts like such a pussy all the attraction is dried up. Just like a woman who gets fat in a relationship. When you're a man who doesn't worship her and is willing to walk away from her is she annoys you it makes you stand out like a shiny gold nugget in a field of manure.

No Woman Is Worth Your Annoyance

Alright I want you to say it with me "No woman is worth my annoyance". Have high standards and always, always, always be ready to "next" a girl. Even if you're married you still need to be able to do this. Not saying to have a stable of mistresses nearby necessarily but rather have the ability to go out and get a girl instantly and always be willing to walk away from the one that you have. She needs to know that you're not going to tolerate any bullshit from her and will put her in her place or replace her entirely if the need should arise. And she should also know that you are totally capable of doing this.

No woman is worth hurting and especially not ruining your quality of life. You only have so much time on this earth. Every moment of it should be spent in a productive way. Always be ready to walk away from any woman and next her. Don't sit there and tolerate bullshit. Some women you're better off calling out and they'll snap into line however others aren't even worth that. Remember no woman is worth your annoyance. Say it out loud with me again "No woman is worth my annoyance, I have too high of value for that". Don't put up with shit from a woman (or anyone really) call them out or replace them. But no matter what always be willing to walk away.

The Abundance Mindset

You need to have the abundance mindset when it comes to women (along with money and other things in life but that's a topic for another time). You have to realize that women aren't that special and in fact are a commodity with a very short shelf life that depreciates rapidly. Also new women come to maturity every single last day of the year. It's a renewable resource. You couldn't sleep with all the beautiful women you wanted to even if you spent the rest of your life doing nothing but sleeping with beautiful women.

Think about that. Even if all you did for the rest of your life was sleep with beautiful women you still couldn't sleep with them all. And there are "men" out there who value the shrew they are with so much they won't even leave her when she cheats, gets ugly, or is a bitch. Talk about pathetic. There are more quality women then any man could ever use. Women are not a scarce or a rare commodity, not even the good looking feminine ones much less the average ones. Stop overvaluing something that's of such low value while undervaluing something that's of immense value (yourself).

Summary

So no matter what always be ready to walk away from a woman. Nothing is worth your pride or honor. Don't take shit from anyone especially a woman. Have pride in yourself and be a man. It doesn't matter if you want to bang a different girl every night, date pretty girls while you work on your goals, or have a woman to raise a family with. No matter what this rule applies. Always be ready to walk away at a moment's notice, you'll never regret it and it leads to healthy proper interactions between you and women.

Women Want To Be Objectified

If you did the complete and utter opposite of what women (especially Feminists) say to do, then you would be more successful than ninety percent of guys out there when it comes to women. Males nowadays have been brainwashed into believing that women are just like them. That they operate rationally, have a sense of honor, and can set their own direction in life. Concepts and ideas that would have been laughable to ninety nine percent of human history and for good reason.

The first step all males must take to become men is to undo this brainwashing.

Women are different than men. These differences stem from our unchangeable biology. The same biology that cavemen had and the same biology that the last man will have. When you understand this underlying basis it'll all make sense. Much of modern thought (and therefore problems) stems from trying to change the unchangeable or even worse pretending that it doesn't exist. You can pretend that the wall in front of you doesn't exist it won't change what happens when you crash into it.

Women Love Being Objectified

Here is a truth that you'll never hear anyone in the mainstream say, women love to be objectified. Not like, but love. Why do you think women have legions of beta orbiters? Because these males shower them with affection and desire and the woman gets her validation from that. As long as a woman knows she is sexually attractive to men she will feel some sense of security (what little a woman can have). A male giving her attention makes her feel good and that she's "still got it".

Of course women use these orbiters and weak males for attention and validation then discard them when/if they finally make their move. Women would much prefer to be objectified and desired by a dominant strong man, whose interest they would reciprocate unlike the weak male. However something is better than nothing. So these women will lead the weak males on and hope that they are sexually attractive enough to attract the attention/desire (i.e. objectification) of a strong powerful man. What we call an alpha male.

Why Is This?

Now you may be wondering why is this? Why do women cry and whine about being objectified but then jump with glee when they are objectified by a strong man? First off never listen to what women say rather watch what they do. That sentence alone could change the dating dynamics of even the most desperate loser. The reason for this all stems from what we talked about in the opening of this chapter, biology. When a woman is sexually objectified she is fulfilling her biological function to a large extent (which is ultimately reproduction).

Remember biology always trumps ideology a woman can say whatever she wants it won't change her biological imperative. A woman who is never objectified because she is not sexually attractive will never reproduce and therefore will feel unfulfilled because she isn't fulfilling her biological role. Ultimately deep down all women want to reproduce with a strong powerful man and bear his children. This is their ultimate fulfillment. Just like a man's would be to be a powerful king with a harem and young nubile women at his beck and call. Remember this is from a biological standpoint, not a moral one.

However the biological standpoint is the strongest of them all.

Women Long For Objectification

Good looking women who age long for the days when men used to objectify them. Women thrive on attention. Of course what they do in response to this attention depends on the type of man you are. If you're a strong dominant man when you objectify her she'll respond by getting horny if you're a thirsty loser then she'll respond with whatever she needs to to keep the attention going or will ignore you if she has better prospects. My point is all women love to be objectified.

To what extent depends on the women but it's one hundred times higher than even the most rational of the mainstream would lead you to believe. Remember never listen to what women say (as it doesn't matter...at all) rather watch what they do and how they respond. Much like they say they hate jerks and love nice guys, want a sensitive man, etc. Any man who follows the advice of a woman will end up having no success with women. Remember women are not logical creatures but rather emotional ones.

Summary

Women like to be objectified because it makes them feel good.

All creatures ultimate goal is reproduction, it is the strongest biological urge under survival (in order to reproduce). When a woman is sexually objectified she knows she has some worth because she can fulfill her biological imperative to some extent. The more strong and powerful the guy the more worth that she will feel. Understand this.

All Women Are Insecure

There are some politically incorrect truths that no matter how hard or long they are screeched against still hold. That fact that all women are insecure is no exception. This has been known to men since the beginning of time yet has been covered up by modern society who constantly works to promote women's self-esteem (which shows how low it naturally is) as well as conveniently ignored by men who wish for a female's nature to be what society says it is and not what it actually is. The fact is all women are insecure.

Now let me get something out of the way at the start. I'm not saying this as a "Ha women are insecure now I get back at those bitches" that would be coming from a place of insecurity and weakness itself. Neither of which have any place in a man's life. As well has from a place of hatred, which as I have said having hatred for women will only destroy you. No, I say this so that you can understand fundamental truths about women because the truth is the only foundation upon which you can successfully base your life.

The truth is the rock and lies the sand. Be the wise man who builds his house on the rock.

The Perception Of Others

Women are controlled by the perception of others. The vast majority of women live their entire lives controlling their reputation and worried about what others think about them. This highlights how women are status first and reality second. Meaning a woman will do whatever so long as her reputation remains intact as that is what she cares about, women do not have a sense of honor like men are capable of having. Of course men can use this part of a woman's psychological makeup to their advantage as well.

This only makes sense as throughout history if a woman was ostracized by the tribe or group she stood no chance of survival. A man can be independent a woman cannot. A man has a chance, even if slim, to survive on his own while a woman has no such chance. Even in our modern society women still rely on men for everything. There never has been and there never will be such a thing as an independent woman. Women are controlled by the opinion of others and cannot survive without the group.

Women Will Fight Tooth And Nail To Hide This

Women are great at saying one thing while acting another. And the sad part is most men fall for it to. Women do not want men to know the truth about them because it would make things inconvenient for women. Knowing that behind all the projecting, anger, bitchiness, makeup, and everything else that there is a scared little girl would throw off the entire game that women have men play. And women cannot have that. Men becoming aware that they are the ones with power is the biggest threat to the game the majority of women play.

Women will vehemently deny being insecure but as the wise sage Shakespeare once said "The lady doth protest too much" meaning that if that were true they wouldn't fight so hard against it. For example a man who is weak will fight accusations of weakness one hundred times harder than a strong man who will laugh or shrug it off. Women will project their insecurity onto others which is why many women are always calling men out on this or that, trying to hide their own insecurities by throwing men off the trail.

All women are insecure. From the hottest girl you can think off to the bitchy Feminist woman with blue hair. All women are still little girls inside but of course will fight tooth and nail so that men will never know this. Which makes sense on a level as many men would take advantage of this. Yet it still remains true.

Fixing A Inflated Market

Women know they are insecure and are aware of their inherent worth. When weak men come along and try to inflate their egos they know it's a fraud. Sure they'll bask in the attention and when a real man calls them out on it, they'll test him to see if he is actually speaking the truth. And when she finds that he is, she will submit to him because he doesn't buy her bullshit. Not buying a woman's bullshit is a huge part of them respecting you and being a masculine man. So when a man calls them on their true worth and not bullshitting them they respond positively to that.

The biggest point I want you to take away from this is that I want you to understand that underneath that mask, whether it is makeup, bitchiness, or anything else is an insecure little girl. So when a woman freaks out on you, you know you have struck the truth. Maintain your frame and let her try to throw you off. When you aren't she will respect you, even if she hates you for exposing the facade for what it is. This isn't to say go around pulling back the curtain on women but simply to show that you understand the true nature of the game. That the wizard behind the curtain is a scared little girl and that all women on some level are little girls, often scared.

All Women Are Insecure

All women are insecure. Say it again, all women are insecure. The hottest of the hot and the frumpiest of the frumpy. All women behind their various masks are little girls and treat them as such. A woman will test you to see if you actually see the game for what it is and are aware of your true value. When they see that you are they will respect and submit to you. You don't have to do anything with that submission and respect if you don't want to but it will be there.

Again this isn't to take advantage of women but rather to make sure you are relating rightly to them. That you are relating as man to woman and you don't fall for their or society's bullshit that is shoved down your throat through the schools, media, and government propaganda. Remember all women are insecure. All women behind their masks are scared little girls. Once you have their submission then take care of them as such and as you see fit. Just understand the underlying dynamic present.

Women Are Easier Than You Think

From the talks of most dating "experts" and guys who pretend to teach men how to have the sex life they want you would think women were these incredibly complicated creatures where you essentially have to become a master at seduction before any are going to open their legs for you. While this is great for selling their high level programs and making lots of money of gullible fools, the truth of the matter is that women for the most part are actually really easy.

Sleeping with women isn't something that requires the equivalent of mastering a martial art, it really requires about as much effort as opening a jar of pickles. As I've said getting laid is easy stop making it hard. Look if you just went up to ten women introduced yourself directly, made your intentions know, and escalated on them at least one of them is going to sleep with you. Women are easy. I don't say this as an insult but rather as a fact. You don't have to be some badass alpha male or whatever to sleep with lots of women, sure it'll help. But as long as you have a pulse and take action you'll be doing better than most men.

The Truth We Want To Deny

The fact of the matter is most men like to think that women are going to make them earn sex. That if they're not super studs then the good looking women are going to turn them down. We like to believe that because we like to think that women are something that they're not. Fact of the matter is many times a woman (even a good looking beautiful "classy" woman) will sleep with some loser she met just because she wants some sex and he was the only one that took action and made himself available. He might not have been her first choice or even her tenth but he's the one that made a move.

Many times women just want sex. If you're some short douche bag who you're friends make fun of but you make moves on women that person will be you and sometimes with beautiful women. How many times have you seen a gorgeous woman leave a club with some shrimpy creepy guy. Alright maybe not every night but it happens, and it happens because why you were trying to be Mr. rich six pack crazy game. He was going up and hitting on women. Because he knows that women are easy.

Women Are Easy

Again we like to pretend they're not and like to think that getting laid (especially with a beautiful woman) is an accomplishment. Sort of like writing a book or making a big sale. But it isn't, it's as much of an accomplishment as brushing your teeth in the morning. We are taught that women value sex highly because then males will work hard to earn the affections of women (making society rich in the process) when the fact of the matter not much effort is required to sleep with lots of women.

You don't have to be rich, jacked, or have great game. You just have to make yourself available and escalate. Just making a move will get you laid more often than the vast majority of men. That's why I recommend that you always go for it. I've seen guys who are skinny, weak, don't know the first thing about game yet get laid more than guys who work on that just because they're always going for it with women they meet. Because they know that women are really easy.

So What To Do

Every beautiful woman that you're putting on a pedestal

thinking that she only goes for certain types of guys has had one night stands with guys you'd make fun of and be shocked if you found that he slept with her while you were sitting in a corner thinking you weren't "good enough". Look let's get something straight by being a man you're already more than good enough for every woman that has ever existed and will ever existed. And if you doubt then you are greatly overvaluing women and should learn more about their psychology and biology. Your opinion will change.

This doesn't mean to not dedicate yourself to self-improvement (of course your goals should be more than sleeping with women, imagine if you greatest goal in life was to open a pickle jar, pretty pathetic right?). Of course if a studly alpha guy is taking action he's going to get more women than the shrimpy nerd. But the point is to take action because of how easy women are. Imagine if you knew that going up to ten women one of them was guaranteed to sleep with you. Well even if you are the biggest of losers but don' overvalue women that's going to be true for you. Women are easy, never forget this.

Summary

The majority of women are easy. Much much easier than you think. If you have a pulse and a functioning dick then you can get laid every weekend. Add good game, looks, and style to the mix and you can get laid every day if you really wanted to. Women will have sex with guys they met five minutes ago just because they're horny. Women are just as easy as men as long as their reputation will remain intact. Stop thinking women aren't easy because they are. Stop overvaluing them and realize they've probably slept with plenty of men you would consider way below you. Including is not especially the beautiful "classy" ones. Never underestimate how easy women are and above all else stop overvaluing them (especially if it's just because they're hot).

A Simple Word That Is A Guaranteed Panty Dropper

What if I told you there was a word that was guaranteed to make a woman's panties drop. A word that when women hear it, it sends shudders down their spine and to other places. You would most likely think "Ha Charles I am no fool, that PUA nonsense doesn't work". And I would agree with you. I'm not talking about some weird NLP trick or to say certain words really loud and point at your junk or whatever it is that has been recommended by PUA losers. No rather I am talking about a word that men used to say all the time but is rarely heard anymore.

I've talked about how women can sense a man's dominance before and this word is a key indicator a man's dominance. Males who never say this word are by definition submissive and weak while men who keep this word at the tip of their tongue are seen and strong and dominant. Not that saying this word in and of itself will make you strong or dominant but rather it's the mindset behind it that counts.

So What Is This Word?

The word is "No". A simple two lettered word yet one that contains immense power. And one that is rarely said or at least rarely said when it's a male interacting with a female. Males have been trained to be "yes men". We've know this for some at least in the office environment but it goes much further beyond that as well. It has permeated every aspect of a male's life. Now not only do we have sackless "Yes "men"" at work but we have the "yes dear" males at home.

Those who live under the rule of a wife who despises them. Who they constantly say yes to and do everything the woman says like an obedient whipped dog. Women hate weak men. This isn't to say that doing nothing for your wife is the right path or that saying "no" to everything will make you a man. Remember it is the mindset behind the words. When you say "no" you show you have standards and that you are a man who will stick to his guns.

Try It Out

Next time someone asks you something I want you to say "no" and see the reaction. Of course if your friend is calling you for drinks because he just got back from Iraq say yes but you get what I mean. Your girlfriend or wife asks you to do something, your parents call you to come to their place to do some work, or a coworker asks you to do something that you know isn't your job or your responsibility. When you give yourself permission to say "no" you embrace another part of your masculine nature and your masculine power.

The more you say "no" the better it will feel. Don't worry you can always say yes, saying yes is easy. Saying "no" actually takes some guts. At first people (especially a woman who thought you were a sap) will react negatively to it. So what? Let them. Eventually they will either go find someone else to pick on or come to respect you. And if it's a woman respect leads to attraction.

Stick To Your Guns

As a man we must stick to our guns. This doesn't mean we never listen to others, we are always open to advice from the wise. But rather this means when we come to an conclusion about something we stick to it unless better knowledge comes our way. Point is we don't change our opinions for others or compromise on our standards. If you don't smoke weed and someone at a parties offers you a hit and you say "no", you stick to your guns. Let them be losers. Again this isn't about doing or not doing drugs, it's about having balls.

Likewise if a woman tells you to carry her bag or do something of that nature say "no". Her friends, family, and all the beta white knights will come against you but it doesn't matter because you are a man and going to remain firm. The white knights are weak and will back down, the women will probably get turned on by you (no matter what they say), and any man worth a damn will come to respect you. And most important of all you keep yourself respect. It's a winning situation no matter how you look at it.

Summary

Saying "no" just for the sake of saying "no" doesn't make you strong or a man. It's the mindset behind it that counts. So don't go around saying "no" to everyone and then saying "No one respects me and they all think I'm an ass". Again remember it's the mindset that counts. Stick to your guns, hold fast to your standards, and always say "no" when "no" is the answer that you should give.

Why You Should Smile & Make Eye Contact With Every Attractive Woman You Pass

There are a few keys to game which once you have down will skyrocket your success. However these things needs to be done often so that they become habits. When they become habits you don't have to think about them. You will be doing attractive things without even thinking about it. Which is great.

For example take body language. Very few people have naturally good dominant body language. However after becoming aware that their body language makes a difference on how others (especially women) react to them they are going to start adjusting their body language. Once it enters into their conscious awareness they can begin changing it and ingraining it as a habit.

However this only happens after continually reminding oneself over time. Do it once and forget it and it will do nothing to you. However repeat it, especially for a predetermined amount of time and it will begin clicking. Like learning anything at first you suck and have to think about every little thing but then as you practice things start happening automatically. Compare the first time you drove in a car to driving now. First time was probably a nerve racking experience and now you can go a whole car ride without consciously thinking about driving.

The Experiment

I want you to perform an experiment that is going to help you see just how many women there are out there and how attractive you are too them. I'm not saying all of them are going to like you and when you start maybe even not the majority. But keep at it and that will soon change.

Here is what I want you to do. For the next seven, fourteen, or twenty one days (your choice) I want you to smile and make eye contact with every attractive woman that you pass. Now if they are with their biker boyfriend it's not required but you get the idea.

When you see an attractive woman you smile and make eye contact with her. At this point you don't even have to approach her (though you should), just smile and make eye contact with her. It sounds simple, and that's because it is. You'll find that many woman respond with attraction to this. Women want to be wanted and when you show then you want them in a confident way (like smiling and making eye contact) they enjoy it and it turns them on.

Attraction

Smiling and eye contact and two things that project masculinity and confidence. Two things that women are obviously crazy over. It shows that you're not scared to look her in the eyes and that you're not scared to show an interest in her. When I first started doing this I was blown away by the response that I got.

This is especially true for men who think that women are scarce when in reality women are abundant. However for many men who have been unsuccessful with women it can be hard to see this. Once they notice how easy it is to get a response from women it makes it much easier to escalate on that response.

Remember getting laid is easy. It's not rocket science. Most men overthink things which is why they end up not getting laid in the first place. You can get laid from this experience. You don't need anything special to do so. Do you have a dick that works? Great, then get out there and get approaching.

See The Results

Once you see the results of this experience it will change your mindset as to how you view women. Guys who think no women are interested in them will see how completely wrong they are. Within a week they will be approaching beautiful women with no problem. Remember getting laid is easy, you don't have to be Mr. Super Stud to get laid a lot. You simply have to have a working dick. Sure somethings help more than others but if you're out there going after it. Your already ahead of ninety percent of the men out there.

When you smile and make eye contact with a girl you are showing her that you are open to sex. And often girls are just looking for a guy to have sex with. That may sound crazy to some of you but it's the truth. Sometimes girls just want to get laid. Put yourself in their view and you'll be surprised (at first) how often that works out for you.

Summary

So remember for the next week or so whenever you see a woman that you are attracted to you are going to

1. Make eye contact with her

2. Smile at her

Do this and be amazed at the response you get. Many women, including beautiful women, go without getting real attention from a guy. Sure they might get cat called as a wimp drives by them or have a guy flatter and buy them things. But not genuine true masculine attention, what they crave. Smile and make eye contact with women and show them you are the man that they have been dreaming about. Then take and ravish them like a man should. You can thank me later.

A Principle To Always Keep In Mind When Seducing Women

While seducing women is not an over complicated matter there are certainly some principles that keeping in mind will make the process much quicker and easier for you. Women love masculine men, they desire to be desired (especially by the aforementioned masculine men), and there are certain traits that they love. No doubt there is an easy way to seduce women and a hard way and it all has to do with making the principles of nature work for you instead of against you.

It's no different than using your mind. Follow the principles lain out and you will go far, fight against them and if you have enough willpower you'll still make it but it will be a much harder row to hoe. We must remember humans are biological creatures and seduction and attraction are based on this biology. Notably the biological differences between men and women. Biology is seduction essentially (as well as masculinity/femininity but that's a discussion for another time).

Turning Women On

I've talked about the differences between the sexes before. One notable difference is that the man is the instigator and the woman the recipient. A male who waits for a woman to make the first move is going to spend many nights with his hand and disappointment as his only companions. A man must be the instigator and the leader. He must be the spark that gets the fire going. A woman is very rarely (especially if attractive) going to. Usually only ugly women and old women are going to be desperate enough to make the first move.

It's the man's job to put the forces of attraction into motion. A woman is rarely going to respond unless the man first shows interest. Maybe eye contact, a smile, or putting herself in close proximity is the extent most women will go too, especially if they are intimidated by you. And honestly if you've been following my writings for any good amount of time, many women are going to be intimidated by you (in a good way). I'm about to dive deeper into one of the most important biological differences between men and women but first want to make sure you understand everything is predicated on the man making the first move and showing interest boldly and forwardly.

Instant Turn On

Men's sex drive is like a light switch. One second there could be nothing the next it could be running full force. Imagine working on some problem on your computer and then you turn around and your girl is naked and spread out on the mattress behind you. You're going to go from 0 to 100 in no time flat. You can go from completely preoccupied to screwing like rabbits in literally thirty seconds. That's how the male sex drive works. It's like a light switch it can be turned on in a second (and turned off as well).

Males often go into seducing women thinking that their sex drive is the same. Now there is no doubt that women want and love sex (especially from masculine men) but their sex drive works very differently. Now women can get turned on much quicker than is commonly believed as well as they want sex much more than is commonly believed. Remember women care about their reputations so pretend like they're not easy when 99% of them are. Keep their reputation in tact and they'll be the sex freaks they've always wanted to be.

Slow Cooker

Women get turned on more like a slow cooker. It takes some time and slowly cranks up. Slow being a relative term compared to male's sexuality. A woman can go from just meeting you to screwing you in under twenty minutes under certain circumstances. Again slow is a relative term but an important difference to keep in mind. Women like being seduced. They like the interplay and being desired. They enjoy the process where the male generally only cares about the end result. Women enjoy the sexual tension that gets developed and then it's ultimate climax in rough sex.

As a man though you must stoke this fire until it rages. You must build it up. Don't get me wrong always be forward, aggressive, and unapologetic about your desires. But understand that a woman takes a little longer to get going. It doesn't take as long as the mainstream would have one believe and romance has nothing to do with it. It has to do with being a man and seducing her. Constantly stoke the fire until it rages as hot as it can and then screw her brains out like she's wanted all night.

Summary

Seduction is an event for men and a process for women. Although it can be a very quick process. Just like there is a process to selling someone there is to seduction. Of course a skilled salesman can move someone through the process almost instantaneously nevertheless the process is still there and in play. Likewise a masculine man can have a woman turned up within a couple of minutes. Just remember be a little bit patient women take longer to get turned on, keep seducing her and everyone will end up with a happy ending. And remember this is all started by you the man showing interest.

Naked Desire

Naked desire. What is naked desire? Naked desire is that deep yearning desire you have for a woman. The one that all men have yet most hide or try to keep pent up. The masculine desire for a woman. That is what I'm talking about. You see your naked desire for a woman plays a key role in seducing and sleeping with women. Desire is an incredibly important yet often overlooked part of having good game and having the sex life that you want. Without naked desire you will be a robot and not have your heart in it, which will lead to lackluster results at best.

Many who preach ineffective methods of game say that you should hide your desire for a woman and never show it. While I understand the basis for this there is a better way. They say this because most men are overeager to please women and lavish their desire on them but from the wrong frame. They do it from the frame of a placating little boy and to get over this many recommend divorcing themselves from their desire and treating women coldly. Again I understand the point behind it but this is still overall an ineffective way of having the sex that you want with the woman that you want.

Naked Desire

When your levels of naked desire are high you naturally go after women, making it very important for good game. Having raw animalistic desire for women turns them on. Remember women want to be wanted, especially by masculine men. When you desire a woman from the frame of a placating boy she may accept the attention but she will never return the desire in a sexual way. Divorcing yourself from your desire for a time may be good in this particular situation but it cannot be the end goal.

You must be in touch with and harness your masculine sexual desire, your naked desire for women to fully interact with them. Women don't get turned on by robots but by men. Men with desire, balls, and passion. Don't divorce yourself from your sexuality like many recommend. Learn to be a man and your sexuality will be something women desire not something that makes them uncomfortable when it comes from the frame of a little boy. Express your true desires for women. Feel it in your bones.

How To Cultivate That Desire

If your strung out, tired, been whacking it to porn three times this week, and have a bad attitude it's going to be hard to have that desire and use it to go after women. Many men numb themselves to life and to their masculine desires. They neuter themselves and shut off their mind, becoming one without desire. They become lifeless without masculine energy. You must reverse this trend that so many men have fallen in. You must cultivate your naked desire for women. Once this is cultivated trust me you'll never need to psyche yourself up to go meet and seduce women, it will come naturally like it's supposed to.

First thing is make sure you are getting in good nutrition. If your dehydrated and low on zinc sexual desire is going to suffer. Stay away from porn and artificial stimulation. Focus your sexual desire on real women in the real world not pixels on a screen or a fantasy in your head. Save your sexual desire to express it to real women in the real world. When you go out don't get excessively drunk, which will prevent you from getting laid more than not. Cultivate that desire and express it to women. Smile at them, interact with them, touch them, trust me they're dying for this. As more and more men retreat into their numbness women are more and more desperate for masculine attention from real men.

Summary

So while divorcing yourself from your desires may be good at the beginning level, there comes a time when it's going to hurt you. You must show your desire to a woman to sleep with her. Let me repeat that you must show your desire to a woman to sleep with her. At some point it must be done, at some point she must know you have a carnal desire for her for anything to happen. "Playing cool" or being "aloof" or whatever can only do so much. At some point you have to find your balls and go for it.

It takes guts to openly show your sexual desire for a woman. Honestly, not hiding it behind something like a little boy. But straightforwardly and without apology like a man. Don't keep your desires down and hide them. Show and express them, show that you are not afraid and are a man. Women crave masculine desire and attention. So go and give them what they want and you will both end up happier in the end. Never hide your desire from a woman, show your naked desire openly and unashamedly.

Why You Should Never Hide Your Interest In A Woman

There is a school of thought in which men recommend to other men to be coy and beat around the bush in regards to seducing women. They advocate just about everything other than actually expressing your masculine desires for the woman. They recommend being friends, being docile, pretending to be gay, asking her opinion on something, asking her about where she bought her shoes (seriously), chopping off your balls. Alright I'm kidding about the last one but that is the essence of their uh "game". This group of men is called men who don't get laid a lot or indirect game.

Now first off let me say indirect game means different things to different people. But if anyone is recommending neutering yourself to get in close to a woman to then suddenly un-neuter yourself they don't know what they are talking about. Women want men, masculine men with masculine desires. Men do not play coy, playing coy is for little girls because its feminine. Becoming more feminine to get laid is like breaking your knees to run a race. It just doesn't make any sense and is the most counter-productive thing you can do.

Cross The Line

When you want to have sex with a woman or even just have a healthy relation with her you must relate to her as man to woman. Not friend to friend, not person to person, but man to woman. If you want to have sex with a woman you must cross the line as in show her your desire and that you want her as more than "just a friend" or whatever. You want her sexually. You will never have sex with a woman if you do not cross the line. Sure crossing the line opens you up to rejection and criticism but if you are a man you should be immune to this or building up that immunity. Having balls opens you up to criticism. Sure if you never cross the line you'll never get rejected but you won't get laid or have fun or be a man or be yourself either.

If you never cross the line you'll never be anything more than friends to women. You have to let your interest be known to a woman. A man doesn't care what others think, say, or do. If he has a desire for a woman he doesn't think "Wait isn't expressing me desire beta...or wait is it alpha…or….” not he finds his balls and goes for it. Let me tell you something right now there is tremendous power in just going for it. It automatically sets you apart from ninety nine percent of guys out there who don't.

Want To Be Wanted

Women want to be wanted. They want men to want them. They feel good when men want them. Not when men leer at them but don't have the balls to say hi, not when they neuter themselves and try to be friends all of the sudden to have desires for her down the line. They want to be wanted by men who have no trouble expressing their desire for a woman. Now many of you are thinking don't men express their desires for a woman all of the time.

The answer is no. Sure a man will whistle or make some remark that he knows will fail so he is off the hook but expressing true honest desire in a masculine way is rare and something women want more than anything. Do this and you'll never have competition. Women are starved for passionate male attention (that is honest and straightforward) like men are starved for beautiful feminine women. Telling men to be indirect to get girls is like telling women to be bitchy to get men. It just doesn't make any sense and ironically is what many "game" books for women do.

Straightforward And Honest

Instead of neutering yourself show women the passion, want, and desire you have for them. Don't give two shits what other insecure men (or women) will think or how will you be judged. If you feel something (including or especially sexual desire) for a woman than express that to her. "But wait wouldn't telling her I want her give her the power and isn't that a compliment and aren't compliments beta. And, and, and"

and shut up. Who cares be a man and express your desires. Trust me it'll work better than anything else. No it's not beta, unless beta means getting laid like tile and having balls (which last I checked it doesn't). Don't get caught up in bullshit, when you see a woman you want express that.

Women are starved for passion. A big reason for this is one that society has done its best to destroy relations between the sexes and too many men numb themselves with porn, work, or something else (women do so also but this chapter is directed or about women). Don't numb the masculine desire out of yourself with artificial stimulation. Don't hide your desire for the woman you want. Express it uninhibitedly and unashamedly to her like a man would. Be honest with women about how you feel about them.

Summary

Being coy and neutering yourself is an excellent way to never get laid or at the very least making it ten times harder than it has to be. Getting laid isn't hard. Be honest with your desires. If you see a woman who you think is sexy and want to see later. Then use this crazy insane pickup line "Hey I thought you were sexy and wanted to see what you are doing later" cue the collective gasp. But…but…but that'd be like…normal. Actually using some indirect weird line or routine would be normal as it takes no balls to do those things. But to express your real and true desires that takes balls and if I know one thing it's that women love balls.

Show your naked, unrestrained, shameless desire. This takes balls and is therefore extremely attractive to women. Be honest with your wants, desires, and intentions with women. Be upfront about what you want. Women already know and it is refreshing and a turn on when a man is honest about it. So have balls and express your masculine desires for women (whatever they may be) honestly and unashamedly. Be forward, be bold, be ballsy, and be direct and you'll never have a problem getting laid. It doesn't matter what others think, only what you want.

Express yourself (including your desires) freely, honestly, openly, unashamedly, straightforwardly, and boldly. You will be the man among boys. You will be the man all women want. You will be in the top one percent of men if you can do this. Now go

out and do it the women of the
world are waiting.

Is Desire The Key To Game?

Attraction and sex are primal things. They go beyond words and phrases. They are a natural and instinctual thing. They have been around since before humans communicated through words written or otherwise. One mistake that I see many make in regards to having lots of sex with beautiful women is that they get in the way of their own primal desires. This is usually done because they listen to some guru market pua who tells them so crap like they should never show a woman desire or something like that. Which effectively stifles that man's natural sexual energy that women crave and plays a big part in whether or not a man and a woman have sex.

Getting laid is not hard or complicated. It is a relatively straightforward process one a man becomes in tune with his masculinity and his masculine desires. Desire is a key component of "game" which is really just naturally relating to the opposite sex as a man. As a man you want a woman, you want her physically. Hiding this does not do you any favors. Being indirect is a great way to either postpone something that would have happened a lot earlier or preventing a sure thing from happening. No matter what when you are indirect and hide your desire for a woman you lose.

Why Desire Matters

A woman has to know you want her. At some point if you're going to sleep with her she has to know that you want too. A normal man would have no problem showing this desire. He would show it in a bold and straightforward way. And no whistling or cat calling is not bold or straightforward as the men use it because they don't have the balls to really approach a woman and assume it will fail most of the time. Showing your masculine desire for a woman unapologetically is going to turn her on like nothing else. Showing that desire through your eyes will have her hypnotized by you.

With desire you will get laid a lot. It's as simple as that. Give a guy the very rudimentary basics of game, hell have him read the chapter on approaching beautiful women and then send him out and with enough desire (as in sexual desire for women) he will start getting laid left and right. Women are easy to men who show them sexual desire unapologetically and in a manly direct way. Meanwhile have a guy who knows everything there is to know about attraction yet watches too much porn or lives at home with his parents and therefore has no desire will not get laid much if at all.

Cultivate Desire

Having desire for woman is a natural thing. However we live in an unnatural society. You have people who will tell you your sexual desires for woman are evil, wrong, or whatever. But it's bullshit, they're naturally and healthy. Combine that with someone who chronically whacks off to porn and suffers the consequences of it. Combine that with a bad diet and it's no wonder that many men have trouble with having the right desire to project to women. The first thing a guy must do is get in touch with that primal masculine desire that is the number one factor in getting laid a lot.

Eating a healthy diet and cutting out crap is a start. Follow that with limiting or completely cutting out masturbation and porn so that your sexual desires aren't being siphoned off but can be applied how they were meant to be applied. To real women. If you live with your parents you need to solve this.

Find ways to make money, work overtime until you save enough to move out, do a side hustle. Anything but if this is your situation your number one goal is to move out before anything else. Being an attractive masculine man isn't going to mean much (or even be fully possible) if you're living in your mom's basement.

Summary

Desire is often overlooked but is one of the most important parts of game. You have got to want it. When you want it you'll get it. It's as simple as that. That primal sexual desire is what is going to do more for you as far as getting laid is concerned than anything else. Showing your true sexual desires to women unapologetically and forwardly is going to turn them on and lead to some fun times for you. Don't hide, push down, or divert your desires. Don't waste it on porn and don't let it never build up by having a horrible diet.

When the desire is there, the way will appear. If you're not getting laid and you're not as put above living with your parents or in some other unfortunate living situation then you need to check your desire. Take some zinc, lay off the masturbation, channel that desire to the women around you.

Use it as energy to fuel you and create sparks between you and the women you are going to meet. That is what it is there for, that is what it was created for, so use it.

A Simple Mind Trick That'll Have You Getting Laid Like Tile In No Time

And no this isn't a mind trick you use on a woman but rather one you use on yourself. Seduction is just as much a mind game as anything else, your mind that is. Meaning that it's much more important to get what's on the inside right then what's on the outside to have the success with women that you want. You don't need to have whatever it is you think you need to have before you can start going after the women you really want. The whole you have to be in shape to get in shape women is all bullshit. Women are attracted to men by internal traits that they exhibit through their behavior while men are attracted women their external traits that they exhibit through their body.

It doesn't work the same for men as it does for women which is why it confuses many men when the skinny guy who hasn't seen the inside of a gym ever is banging girls he's been working on the gym for years to get while he has nothing to show for it. If you have a dick then you can already sleep with the women that you want if you follow what's outlined here. Not that outside things don't help because they do but they shouldn't what you focus on. Get in shape for your own health and get rich for your own life, don't do either to get women as there are much more effective and time saving paths.

You're Already Enough

First and foremost you're already enough for any woman. Simply by the fact that you are a man you are enough for any woman. I don't care if you live in your parents basement and are skinny beautiful women will still sleep with you. I've seen men having nothing going for them but still sleeping with beautiful woman simply because they had the mindset that they were enough and therefore they were. Women don't work like men. If a fat chick went around thinking "I am enough" it wouldn't do anything to raise her attractiveness or get the sex life she wants. Mind is the master for men.

Now this doesn't mean you shouldn't develop your life, you absolutely should. But do it for yourself not to sleep with beautiful women. You already have everything you need for that.

Beautiful women will sleep with ugly losers from time to time just because they're there and they put themselves out there. Even the most dedicated bodybuilder has missed a day of training here and there, well it's the same with beautiful women. Every one of them has had that night when they just wanted to get laid and did even if it wasn't their "ideal choice".

Am I X Enough?

One of the worst things I've seen that messes guys up with women is using the whole 1-10 scale. Not judging women by it which is whatever but matching themselves up with the women.

First off as I said above attraction for women is different than attraction for men. They think "Oh I am guy 7 and therefore can sleep with women 7's and above". This is the dumbest bullshit ever for a variety of reasons (too many to list here). Remember you are already more than enough. You have to really get this drilled down deep. You are a man and are therefore more than enough for any woman.

You don't have to be more X. You don't have to be what you define as attractive. I know this is going to be hard for many to get because of how much effort they put into getting girls through nondirect means. Getting in shape, dressing better, getting status, and everything else. While those things help if your only goal is to get women they are not the best use of your time. Do those things for yourself. To get women you are more than enough. You are male they are female. That's all you need to sleep with the most beautiful women. You don't need anything outside of yourself.

Action Is King

In life and in seduction. Simply by approaching a woman and showing your interest to her you are going to be in the top ten percent of men because of your boldness and confidence. I don't care how you look. And guess what showing this boldness and confidence is going to cause massive amounts of attraction in the woman, so much so that she may even get nervous and walk away. Like if a smoking hot chick walked up and started talking to the average guy he wouldn't know what to do with himself. It's the same with women.

Others may start testing you, even give you a look of sheer horror. Doesn't matter women react in different ways (and illogically) to being approached. She could be crazy attracted by walk away saying "you're gross" but want you badly. I know you're saying "But that doesn't make any sense Sledge" and you're right. But since when the hell have women made sense in a logical way??? Never that's when. If you approach her she's attracted to you. Simply by approaching her you become the most high value man and more high value than her. It's as simple as that. Just hold the frame and she'll be yours.

Summary

Approaching makes you the hot chick and the girl the nervous guy. Remember it doesn't matter what she says or does, simply hold

the frame and she'll be yours.
She'll thank you later. Remember
she's not going to act rationally just
be the man and everything falls into
place. Simply take the action and
you'll be ahead of the vast majority
of guys out there. Women are
attracted to men through their
actions and frame. Don't forget this
and use it to your advantage. Also
always realize you are already
more than enough for any woman.

How To Use Emotional Spiking To Get Laid

Women are controlled and led by their emotions, there is no doubting or disputing this. Sure many men and women would like to think otherwise and think that women are just as logical and deductive as men but even the most career oriented bitchy Feminist is at the end of the day still a woman. Therefore she still has the biology of a woman and will respond to things in a womanly way, no matter how hard she tries to suppress her own biology. It's inevitable.

Women love feeling emotions and when a guy (especially a masculine guy) can spike her emotions she'll be his. One of the key tenets of what we call game is emotional spiking. Meaning making a woman feel strong emotions. So a woman goes from being bored and emotionless to all of the sudden responding strongly to something that you have said or done. This is also know as teasing or busting her chops. And it's a fundamental part of getting laid a lot.

Emotional Tension

Like I said above women love feeling strong emotions, they are after all emotional creatures. They are led and swayed by their emotions the same way that a man can be led and swayed by logical and reason or a nice ass. When you do things that cause emotional spiking with a women such as busting her chops (with a smile on your face) she is going to feel things in response to that. This is going to create emotional tension.

The great thing about emotion tension is that it is tension and tension translates into other things. For example when a woman says she likes a certain band or whatever are you respond with "They suck" with a big smile on your face she is going to respond positively. She is used to the boring guy agreeing with her and nodding his head as he gets to know her. Here you do something very different from that. Emotion tension will translate into sexual tension if you are a masculine man. So be sure to cause emotional tension by using emotional spiking.

Tease Her Playfully

You've probably heard before to tease women playfully or to treat her like a bratty little sister. Pretty much means to bust her chops or to cause emotional spiking. You don't let her get away with anything and are poking her with your words to get a reaction. The key is to "insult" her while having a big smile or your face. Put another way to put her down but in a good natured way.

A key in this is that you're not doing it to hurt her, you're doing it to cause emotional spiking. You're doing it to tease and play with her in a fun way. You're not trying to hurt her. The words you say are going to come out mean but your intention will be playful. And intentions mean a hell of a lot more than words.

For example say your buddy throws a bucket of cold water on you in the shower and you tell him you're going to kill him. Obviously you're not going to actually kill him as the words don't matter much but the meaning behind the words do. So for example if she asks if she looks hot in her dress and you point your finger down your throat like you're going to puke but then smile she's going to call you an ass (but with a giant smile on her face).

When To Use

This works on the vast majority of women but there are some who will not respond well to it. For example traditional feminine women sometimes will get hurt as they genuinely like you and are confused by it. Even if you make it clear you are kidding (which they will then be okay with) probably not best to continue busting their chops as you would with other women. This works like a charm on bitchy Western women. While it has varying effectiveness on sweet traditional girls. Genuine compliments can work on girls who have not been corrupted by Western society. Again not saying you can't tease them just that to do so less and make sure to calibrate.

It seems to be the more masculinized a woman is as in demeanor because you wouldn't hit on a girl with masculine looks (I hope). The better she responds to being teased, especially the stronger you do it. Don't get me wrong all girls want to be teased to some extent and all girls want to feel emotions, I'm just talking relative here. Like someone one said women communicate by compliments and men by insults. These bitchy women at the club try to be men in their minds (but women in their bodies) and therefore respond better to this form of communication. While the sheltered rural girl (who is also smoking hot) is going to be confused or a bit offended if you started off busting her chops. Because she is feminine in both mind and body. Not saying she'll respond to doting because no women does just saying she'll respond differently to teasing. Food for thought.

Another thing is that the hottest girls usually have lower opinions of themselves than girls in the middle tiers. For example your typical nine or ten is going to get far less male attention than your typical six or seven. At least directly. And being women these nines and tens are going to think that there is something wrong with them. While the six and sevens are going to bask in the attention of thirsty males boosting their ego.

Raising their own far out of proportional while the nine and tens are going to not get much male attention dropping theirs out of proportion as well.

Summary

The point is to utilize emotional spiking. When you spike her emotions and make her feel either positive or negative emotions. She's going to enjoy it. Like I said women are emotional creatures. She would rather have a guy who makes her feel bad than have a guy who makes her feel nothing. Make her feel a range of emotions and she will love you for it. Do this in addition to being masculine and you'll never have any women trouble again.

Make her feel things. Frustrate her and throw her the occasional compliment just to throw her off. When you see a woman walk up to her and playfully begin teasing her. Have a great attitude and a smile on your face, start off busting her chops. It will make you stand out and arouse her emotions instantly. Make fun of something is doing, wearing, or saying but again with a huge smile on your face. Tease her playfully.

A Surprising Truth Women Will Never Admit Too

What women want is not a politically correct subject. As a matter of fact the truth about women is anything but politically correct. From every corner of our society from TV shows, the music, to teachers, to preachers, to your own family the wrong advice is given as to what women want. You'll hear things like "respect" or "love" or "a nice guy" yet anyone with eyes that work can see differently. Obviously there is a large disconnect between what we are told women want and what they actually want.

Listen to the average Feminist (if you dare) and you'll hear time and time again how objectification of women is the worst thing that's ever happened ever and it makes you literally Hitler or whoever SJWs have their panties in a wad about at the moment. If listening to advice about women from normal women is bad then listening to advice about women from SJW/Feminist women is even worse. It would be like going to mentally insane person for life advice.

The Truth That Women Will Never Admit

Women have a game to play. Remember a woman's reputation matters more to her than just about anything. Keep a woman's reputation intact and she'll do just about anything. Because of this many women are loathe to go against society or others. They'll parrot the talking points and party lines simply because they do not want to stand out. Women cannot survive on their own unlike men, making them very sensitive to anything that can ruin their standing with the group.

Being truthful about their sexuality is one of those things. In particular what they like and desire. One thing that all women like and desire is to be objectified. Of course they want to be objectified by masculine men not weak nerds but that should be obvious. Every woman has the desire to be objectified, to be looked at as a sexual object by a strong dominant man and used as one. The only women who get mad about objectification are women who are either not getting objectified by men or getting objectified by weak males.

All women want to be desired by men. Remember women want to be wanted, they want to be desired. They want men to have a visceral desire for them. They want to get lost in their man's dominance and be used by him as he pleases. This is a natural and healthy desire for a woman to have just like it is a healthy and normal desire for a woman to want to possess his woman and use her as a sexual object in the bedroom.

Made For Your Pleasure

Don't be like most males who think showing any sexual interest in a woman is bad. Who go around hiding their want and desire for a woman. Neutering themselves to go along with what Feminists (and some PUAs) say women want. That to talk about sex or bring up sex at all is bad. Women want and desire sex, and often go unfulfilled. Women were in many ways created for a man's pleasure and are unfulfilled when they are not meeting that natural desire. They want to please a man.

In sexual and other ways. When don't show their sexual desire for women and women don't find masculine men to be used by, everyone loses. When I say used I don't mean taken advantage off rather to use as in properly use something. For example when you use a gun to shoot a deer. You aren't taking advantage of the gun nor are you abusing it, you're using it as it's proper function. It's the same for women as one of their proper functions is to be used by their man sexually, in other words to be objectified.

Women were made for your pleasure. Women want to be a man's sexual plaything. Women who are mad about this are women who aren't attractive and feminine enough to be used by men. It would be like dirty old shoes being mad at nice clean ones because the owner used the nice clean shoes much more than the dirty old ones. It's jealousy plain and simple. Do not conform your life view to the view of a bunch of angry jealous women. Woman was made to serve and please man.

Summary

No doubt this ruffled some feathers. So be it, the truth is the truth and that is all that matters. You as a man should never apologize for your natural healthy desires and women should not be ashamed to indulge in their natural healthy desires. Men will objectify women and women want to be objectified in the right context. It isn't evil, wrong, or bad as angry bitter woman would lead you to believe. It's natural, healthy, and desired by both men and women.

Women want to be objectified but will never admit to it. They want to be wanted. All women want attention, especially sexual attention from masculine men. It has always been this way and it will always be this way. Stop feeling bad for going against the wishes of our psychotic society. Remember this quote by the wise Roman emperor Marcus Aurelius "The object of life is not to be on the side of the majority, but to escape finding oneself in the ranks of the insane."

Five Minutes Of Alpha

Never has it been better to be an alpha and never has it been worse to be a beta. In today's world the men at the top of the sexual pyramid are experiencing more success than ever before while those at the bottom are settling more than ever before.

With women's sexuality let out of the bag and unrestrained, society has changed drastically. Women leave their beta husbands for a chance at an alpha in record numbers, women will cheat at the drop of a hat if it's with an attractive guy. To be a man that women fantasize about a man simple needs to be an alpha. Meaning a man who has embraced his masculinity fully and completely as well as understands the truth about women.

You see an guy who is an alpha (a guy who is a man) will stand out in a woman's mind and she will do anything to be with a man that affects her in such a way. The beta's (guy who isn't masculine) money, looks, status, or anything else will not prevent that women he wants or loves from being pumped and dumped by the alpha that she fantasizes about. A guy who gets a woman hot and horny with his masculinity and dominance is going to be her first pick over any other guy no matter what. It doesn't matter if that guy has been dutifully married to her for ten years, had four kids with her, is a ripped millionaire, or anything else.

Five Minutes Of Alpha Is Worth A Lifetime Of Beta

The popular saying five minutes of alpha is worth a lifetime of beta essentially means a woman would rather get banged (or even be around) an alpha guy for five minutes than have a lifetime of devotion, love, or anything else from a beta. The guy who burnt a woman in high school will stand out more than her famous actor boyfriend. Because he is alpha. A guy who doesn't take crap from a woman and puts her in her place is going to stand out in her mind forever more.

The bad boy that dumped her she will still be remembering and fantasizing about ten years down the line, unless a bigger alpha comes into her life. The man who makes the biggest impact on her will crowd out all other men in her life, even if she marries, dates, or whatevers with those other men. She cannot forget the alpha, she cannot shake the tingles that he still stirs up. Women automatically respond this way to dominant men, even though they may hate and/or deny it.

To Be The Alpha Women Fantasize About

To be the alpha essentially means to be a man fully and completely. To be dominant, unapologetic, and strong. To never apologize for your masculinity and to always put yourself first. Women would rather share an alpha man. A man who has his own thing going and for which she is just an accessory to his life that can be discarded and replaced at women.

Then have complete devotion and love from a beta male. A male who is going to put her above himself and who has not embraced his masculinity.

Being and becoming a man is a multifaceted topic and one that is not going to be completely covered in a chapter. Which is why I wrote a book about it, yet even then masculinity cannot be contained with one book. This chapter is to simply show you the direction in which you should go. Put yourself first and the women will come. Work on yourself and invest in yourself. Learn all that you can about being a man and embracing your masculinity. Things like dressing well and looking good are simply stepping stones to become the man you want to be, not the end goal.

Some Guidelines To Get You Started

Be a man completely and without apology. Be dominant. Assert yourself into the world around you. Remember you are man, creation and women are reactive forces you are the active force. Go and make the world to how you see fit. Take the lead with women and in life. Remember the end goal is to become a masculine man. To fully develop that masculinity within you and to understand the nature of women. Do these two things and women will fall at your feet.

Understand how women view you. They are either going to see you as completely irrelevant to them, a good target to take advantage of, or a man they want to submit to and be ravished by. Be strong, dominant, and never let a woman control you. They want you to be the uncontrollable stallion that they pine after. Don't be the donkey for carrying their goods. Be a masculine man and you will be the man women fantasize about. Fully embracing one's masculinity is something that can be developed for a lifetime and is worth doing so. That is your mission and it is the woman's mission to go after a man like you.

How To Game As A High Value Man

Most pickup/attract women advice is given from the paradigm of a complete loser. From a guy who is even lower than your average guy on the street. Have you seen most pickup artists? They're nerdy, scrawny, weirdos. Therefore the advice they give is generally going to be from the paradigm of a nerdy, scrawny, weirdo. Hence things like indirect game, openers, and other stupid shit that the normal guy (much less a guy who has dedicated himself to self-improvement) needs. Hence why pickup looks and feels so weird to the average normal guy and very weird to the successful guy.

I'm not saying all "pickup" advice is bad by the way obviously there is plenty of good advice out there. But the traditional wear a fuzzy hat and ask girl random questions shit and those that imitate them is doing no one but the biggest of losers any favors. Once you become high value (if you've been reading this book you're probably already there) then things aren't different. Girls are easy, seriously they are. They want and love sex, especially with a masculine guy. Don't over-complicate this stuff.

High Value

Simply by approaching a woman and stating your intent directly you become a high value man. It would be like if a fat chick could walk up to you and turn into a stunning gorgeous blond measuring 36-24-36 with long hair, full lips, and a breathy voice. That's the power that us guys have. Think about this most guys will never approach a woman in their entire life. By doing so you are putting yourself in the top ten percent of men out there.

Now granted if you walk up to a girl with yours eyes downcast and mumble out a nervous "Hey" that's not going to make you high value. But if you approach directly like a man looking straight at the girl with a smile then you're golden. Add that on to the rest of your self-development and you're essentially using a nuke where a firecracker would get the job done. You're already way more than enough.

You're The Hot Girl

Alright I want you to imagine a group of average guys in a circle. They have average bodies, average thoughts, and average lives. Now I want you to imagine that blond described above walking up to them and flirting. What would happen? They guy would probably shit his pants, mumble something nervously, or run away. He wouldn't reciprocate because he wouldn't know how. At best he'd sit there speechless or mumble a nervous "Hi" before looking away nervously. Well when you're a high value man (and remember simply approaching makes you one) then this is how many women will perceive you.

When you're a high value man you become the hot chick. Girls will get nervous when you show interest directly (all but the ones with tons of experience) even if they want you to bang their brains out. They'll not know what to do some will act bitchy simply because they're nervous and it came out while others will mutter some things and then walk away. Remember all women are insecure so this will come out in different ways. Don't look for logic in it just understand they're nervous and that'll express itself uniquely to each one.

What To Do

You have to realize you're probably breaking her frame of reality. Manly guys are in short supply and one coming up and expressing his interest directly in her seems too good to be true. You're going to have to calm her down a little bit and get her to relax around you. Be patient with her and you might have to approach her again later if she walks away nervously. It might just be too much for her to take at one time. She might shit test you mildly just because she doesn't know what else to do.

Handle it as you always would (smile and laugh lightly dismissing it for example) and be patient with her. Smile, make lots of eye contact, and give her time to know that this is the real thing and really happening. Here's a good way to think of it. Imagine a peasant girl coming before her king. The vast majority of women are going to be nervous even though they desperately want the king. The difference between the peasant girl and the king, is going to be the difference between you and the average woman. It might take here awhile to get that a guy such as you would have anything to do with someone like her. Just be patient she'll eventually get it.

Summary

The principles and fundamentals all stay the same after all biology doesn't change. But when you become high value some things do change. While all women say they want a masculine dashing man most would go numb if one actually approached them same with men saying they want a loose gorgeous woman. Most would shit their pants if one came up to them. Give the woman time to get that you're interested in her and that this is happening. Once she gets it then the fun really begins.

A Guaranteed Way To Get Laid More Than Ever Before

Alright so if you're like pretty much any other single guy on the face of this earth getting laid more is going to be in your top list of priorities. There are many different theories as to what attracts women to men and a whole host of different systems, philosophies, and other lines of thinking as to what the best way to do this is. And truth be told a whole hell of a lot of them work (after all it's not rocket science, it's getting laid). With that being said there are guaranteed ways to increase how much you get laid.

Certain principles that when followed are going to get you in the sack with a lot more women. Getting laid is something that can be very complicated or very simply depending on what you want. Most guys just want to get their dick wet more with girls that wouldn't make them ashamed and that's pretty much it. And to get that is really easy. It may be something else sleeping with the most beautiful women but for a guy who just wants to get laid more with some decent girls then this chapter will give you all you need.

Put Your Best Foot Forward

First things first while looks and style aren't the end all be all they do give you points in your favor. So might as well take advantage of them. Make sure you are looking your best when you go out. Put some effort into how you look to the world trust me girls will notice. Don't wear a T-shirt and old jeans actually look nice. Throw on some nice jeans, with leather shoes, and a polo as a minimum. Other nice venues in big cities you'll want to upgrade even more and wear a suit.

But even if you're going to the local dive bar look nice. Like I said no old converse and worn out T-shirts. The nice jeans, leather shoes, and polo is the absolute minimum wherever you go. And make sure that they fit nice and look good on you. Buy some nice clothes yourself if you have to, but make sure they fit. Better to have a nice fitting T-shirt than a polo that's 2 sizes too big and droops on you or one that's too tight and becomes a belly shirt whenever you raise you arm above your stomach. Make sure to shower, shave, and have a decent haircut.

Just Do It

Alright now what I want you to do is smile and smile all the damn time. Also I want you to make eye contact with all the women at the bar. Smile and make eye contact with every woman you come across. Then I want you to go up and say "Hi" to women you find attractive. Don't think about how the interaction is going to go, don't worry about how you're coming across, don't worry about if you need an "opener" or some other nonsense. Simply go up and say "Hi" and start talking to women. That's the only thing you should concern yourself with is saying "Hi". Simply making the approach shows you have balls and are an attractive man.

Flirt with her and make things physical, if she's not about it then move on to the next. It's as simple as that. Here's the thing don't sit back and start to overthink things, just take action. Simply by talking to girls you want you're going to keep the momentum going. Approach and escalate and if it doesn't work then move on to the next one. You're going to stand out simply by taking action. Approaching women is going to make you attractive to them. Just keep going until you take one home.

Increase Your Numbers

Like I said it isn't exactly rocket science. The more girls you talk to and escalate on the more girls you are going to sleep with. It's as simple as that. It's a numbers game in many ways. Not that you should focus on this as this causes people to chase certain numbers instead of simply naturally going with the interact they are with. Plus you can always make things work more in your favor, never rely on numbers alone. Simply wanted to point out it's a direct correlation between the number of girls you approach and escalate on and the number of girls you sleep with.

Look good, smile, make eye contact, approach, escalate, rinse and repeat. This will get you laid more than any complicated theory or advanced algorithm. Like I said getting laid isn't rocket science, it's a basic biological function that people vastly over complicate. Follow what I've lain out here and you'll do just fine. You'll naturally learn to adjust and calibrate as you go. Don't worry about problems that aren't there and don't create problems for yourself that didn't exist in the first place. Simply take action and things will fall in line.

Summary

Action is what is going to get you the results that you want. Focus on what you can control (the level of action you take) and everything else will fall in line. Don't worry about the girls potential reaction, just worry about if you are taking action or not. Take enough action and you'll get the results that you want. That's really all there is to it. And this applies to a lot more than just getting laid. It applies to business and other facets of life as well. So taking action should be the only thing on your mind, don't worry about anything else.

Never Forget There's More Than One Way To Skin A Cat

So when it comes to picking up girls, getting rich, getting jacked, or really anything else in life there are generally as many theories are there are successful people doing it (if not more). One person says that picking up girls is all about learning game another says that nah it's all about being a man of value, while another says it's only about looks and status. And so on and so forth. Likewise with getting ripped one guy says it's all about calories in and calories out, another says that it's about quality of those calories, while another says that its about total energy expenditure. And so on and so forth.

Then you look at these guys (we're no counting the charlatans, which there are plenty of especially in these three categories). All of the guys telling you different ways to get girls are pretty successful themselves with girls likewise all of the different trainers are all pretty ripped. Again let's assume these guys are legit and they don't use paid models in their videos and that they're not on gear. They're all telling you something different and yet they're all getting the results that you want. What's up with this?

What It Comes Down To

The fact of the matter is there is more than one way to do something. There is more than one way to get rich, to pick up girls, to get ripped, and anything else in life. Put another way there is more than one way to skin a cat. Success in any endeavor isn't an either or proposition. There are guys who have gained success from a multitude of different ways, many through contradicting paths. Not everyone is going to follow the same exact path as someone who is successful for a multitude of reasons. When you understand this it frees you up to follow your own path and not get bogged down by conflicting information.

It speeds up your progress tremendously as you realize that there is more than one way to get what it is you want. There is more than one way to achieve the success that you want in life. There is more than one way to be a winner and achieve greatness. Don't worry about conflicting advice or if you don't feel the exact same way as someone who you admire. Look at blogging some get their success through marketing their blog, others through putting out enough content that they reach far and wide, while others from networking with bigger bloggers and getting status from them. All different ways to skin a cat yet in the end the cat is still skinned and that's what matters.

What To Look For

So when you are out there looking for ways to succeed and get ahead here is what you do when you run into conflicting advice or when it seems like everyone is saying something different. First and foremost you look for similarities between what everyone is saying. If these people are all successful what are the common points that they all talk about. For example if it's about getting rich I guarantee that they all learned sales and read a ton. Something that from what I've seen are two things every rich person has mastered. Alright not every but ninety plus percent.

What you're looking for is common principles between the successful. Don't focus on the small things that make them different look at the common things that make them all successful. Maybe one is six foot but another is under five foot. Maybe one was born in New York and another in Kentucky. One is white and one is black. These things don't matter, what matters it the common principles that tie them all together. The successful in all fields share traits and principles, these are what you're looking for.

An Example

We'll use picking up girls as an example as it is the topic of this book and will always be a popular topic. From stealing a wife with your best man from a neighboring tribe to picking up girls on Tinder, men will always have an interest in this. Alright not let's say that we have one guy who talks about how you'll only get girls if you're ripped and dress like a boss. Then we have another guy who says that it's all about spiking a girls emotions and being seen as the bad boy. Perhaps they even talk about how the other school of thought is stupid and for losers.

Maybe the ripped guy uses example of nerdy PUAs getting rejected by girls left and right. Meanwhile the bad boy guy uses examples of jacked guys in suits with no game as he steals girls from them. And if we're being honest we can admit that they both have good points. Of course being good looking and dressing nice is going to help with sleeping with the women you want. Likewise we all know good looking well-dressed guys who couldn't get laid to save their lives. Also who hasn't looked at some scrawny PUA type guy and laughed as he gets rejection after rejection. Likewise we see guys who are unimpressive on the outside yet sleep with some beautiful woman.

The Conclusion

So you come to the conclusion, one is that they both have points (as most who are successful do). On the surface (tactics level) they may seem to contradict each other but on a deeper level (principles) they may be talking about similar things and remember they are simply sharing what worked for them. And putting down others is a common marketing ploy (even if you don't know you're doing it). The whole us vs them deal.

What you should first do is look at what they are doing similarly. Alright they're both aggressive, they both have masculine vibes, and honestly if the ripped guy worked on spiking a woman's emotions a little more he'd be doing a little better. Likewise if the bad boy guy spent some time in the gym he'd probably be doing a little better as well. Remember the great Bruce Lee quote "Absorb what is useful, discard what is useless" and look for commonalities over differences.

About The Author

Enjoyed the content? Then could you do me a favor? Leave a review on Amazon or tell a friend about the ways that the book has helped you. I love reading how my books have positively affected the lives of my readers. I read each and every review, they mean a lot to me. If you want to learn more I run a blog at charlessledge.com where you can find more content to further your masculine development to new heights. If you found value in the book drop by and join the community. Looking forward to hearing from you.

-Charles Sledge

Made in the USA
Middletown, DE
07 October 2023

40402550R00295